PRINTHOUSE BOOKS PRESENTS

FATAL TRUCE

Fiction

April Black

VIP INK Publishing Group, Inc.

Atlanta, GA.

©April Black; 2015

PrintHouse Books, Atlanta, GA.

Published : 10-15-15

www.PrintHouseBooks.com

VIP INK Publishing Group; Incorporated

Cover art, designed by SK7.

Editor: Cheryl Hinton

ISBN: 978-0-9965701-9-0

Library of Congress Cataloging-in-Publication Data

#2015952321

1. Urban Literature 2. Drama
2. Crime 4.April Black 5.Suspense

Printed in the United States of America

This is dedicated to my Nana, Maggie Williams. One of the sweetest and unselfish women I've ever known. I love you and miss you dearly. To my first love, my father, James O. Black, may you Rest in Peace. To my mother, Juanita Black, who has always been there and my children who have given me the strength and courage to navigate through this thing we call "Life". I will always love you all.

April

A tale of broken dreams, broken promises, and broken lives pieced together with fortitude, in the midst of moral decay. All that's left is a glimmer of hope that tomorrow will be better, then for a moment it is well, and the universe is at peace. And just at daybreak life orchestrates this, cruel and strategically, debilitating game once more...

Dre grows from a boy into manhood in a way no child should have to; but too often must. With a pocket full of dashed hopes and broken dreams he manages to protect those he loves by any means possible. It is an unusually cruel real life game of chess where the stakes are life and death.

Table of Contents:

THE PROMISE

The smell of fresh cut flowers filled the air. The sounds of mourning could be heard from three blocks away. A dark cloud hovers over the still-shocked St. Johns Missionary Baptist Church congregation, for today they bury two of their own.

(One week earlier) "Not a cloud in the sky, a perfect day for a birthday party," said Desiree Snipes, a 37-year-old fifth grade teacher at Coconut Grove Elementary School. "Get the lead out birthday boy, the guests will be arriving soon. Dre...what are you doing up there boy?"

"Ma, come on now ...I ain't wearing this stupid tie. It's a party, not a recital," yelled Andre through the bathroom door.

"Boy if you don't get your ass out of the bathroom before I count to three, it's going to be a wake in here today!" Desiree, standing only 4'11" is not the one to be playing with and Andre knows this. Slowly he comes out of the bathroom wearing a brown striped bow tie that his grandmother bought him. "You know Nana wants you to look handsome for your 13th birthday party," smiled Desiree as she straightened his tie. Andre still frowned as she kissed his forehead. Let's make a deal, as long as Nana is here you must wear it, but as soon as she leaves to go to bible study, you can take it off."

"Okay...dawg," Dre said while sucking his teeth. "Now give your momma a kiss and let's finish these decorations now before I get mad. Your father and Kiki will be back from the store in a minute." Dre's stepfather, James Snipes and his 4-year-old sister went out earlier to do some last minute shopping for Dre. James had been promising his son a hunting trip for some time now, so he brought Dre his very own rifle bb gun.

James, a self-employed realtor in the South Miami area, father of four, and devoted husband, never got the chance to give his son his present. Less than two miles away from their house tragedy unfolded. As he started into a busy intersection in his gray Camero, a black pickup truck runs a red light and slams into the right side of him sending the two vehicles up in flames. When the smoke cleared, little Kiki was still sitting in her car seat, holding a charred gift that she had picked out herself for her brother; her body was partly dismembered due to the force of the explosion and her little lace party dress singed to her skin. James, however, survived the blast but had serious burns over 90% of his body. Paramedics worked furiously to keep him alive.

The party has already begun. Desiree was beginning to worry about her husband and baby girl when the phone rang. It was Larry Johns, her neighbor and highway patrol, "Hello Desiree…There's been an accident…its James…he needs you Desiree…it's bad."

"Nooooo," she screamed.

"Desiree, we're at Dade County Medical…hurry!"

When Desiree and her children reached the hospital Larry was waiting for them outside. She fell to the floor when Larry told her about Kiki. Dre knelt down to try and help Larry console his frantic mother.

"You got to be strong man…for your mother," he softly tells Dre. "Your dad needs you in there, all of you. He's fighting for his life," said Larry as he escorted the family into the intensive care unit.

For nearly an hour no one said a word. Desiree and her other three children, Dre and his two younger sisters DeeDee and Shannon, quietly surrounded the bedside of her dying husband. She had been given a sedative to make her relax but her tears were a never-ending stream of guilt and anger. For if she had never sent her husband to the store this would not have happened. Her frail and nervous hands tried to hold on to her husband's fading life.

"Hold on baby...oh baby, hold on. Please God don't take him from us too...please God!" Suddenly she felt his hand begin to move. "James, can you hear me," she screamed. He gasped in pain as he was trying to speak. A faint sound came from him, "Auh...Ki...Ki...auh."

His eyes were barely opened but he could still make out his wife's face. The fire had scorched off all of his facial hair as well as the hair on his head. He was covered in bandages. Desiree pulled herself closer to his face and gave him a tender kiss.

"Oh sweetheart, don't try to talk. Everything is going to be fine...we love you honey," she wept.

"The...ba...by, the...baby," he uttered. Desiree hesitated. She had not yet accepted her baby's death herself, but she knew he deserved an answer. Her voice began to tremble with emotion, her eyes dropped to the floor. James although weak and in extreme pain could sense all the emotion in as she broke down.

"Oh…my God…not my sweet ba…by why, why…why," she screamed as she laid her head on his chest. He reached for her as he began to weep silently.

"I'm…soooorry…I didn't…mean to," he said as Desiree quickly interrupted him, "…it's not your fault." Dre and his younger sister DeeDee could not contain themselves any longer. Their silent weeps turned into wails of pain. They threw themselves upon the bed of their father, "Please daddy don't leave us."

Larry, who had been standing in the hallway rushed in to try to console the children who were becoming hysterical. DeeDee, only a year younger than Dre was taking this the hardest. She had always been very close to her father and was terrified that he may die like her sister. James began to caress his daughters hair hoping it would ease her from crying, as he looked up for his only son.

"…Son."

Tearfully, "Yes pops...I'm here," he said as he moved closer so that James could see him. Although James was not his biological father, they were inseparable. Dre's real father had never taken part in his life; as a matter of fact he had never seen him. The only thing his father had ever given him was his name, "Lanier." Desiree married James when Dre was a little over a year old; she was four months pregnant with DeeDee. About five years later Shannon arrived, followed by Kiki only a couple of years later.

James looked up and saw Dre crying.
"Come on...man, I...need you...to be...strong for me now. I don't think I'm getting...out...out of this...one, man. Can I de...pend on you," said James as he continued to struggle with his breathing and it was apparent that he was having a hard time speaking.

"No Pops, you got to get better. I won't let you die," he screamed as he kneeled down beside the bed. "You have to get better; you have to take care of mom. Who's going to take care of mom? Who's going to take me hunting next week," he cried. Larry reached down and touched Dre on his shoulders. James knew he would never leave that hospital alive. He made Dre promise that he would step up and take care of his mom and sisters for him. He told him he wanted him to take his place and be the "man of the house."

Early the next morning, James slipped into a coma. A few hours later he died with his wife and children by his side.

The choir never sang lovelier than that morning. Reverend Magee gave a moving eulogy. Every seat filled in the church, every eye teary. A double funeral, nothing could be more sorrowful. Little Kiki was dressed like an angel wearing a white satin dress full of lace. Desiree made it herself to try to keep preoccupied that week. Since the baby's hair had been partly burned off, she wore a beautiful white bonnet. Desiree demanded, "Mr. BoBo," her stuffed penguin be buried with her. Kiki had to sleep with him every night or she had a fit. He was very worn and one of his eyes was missing, but she loved him to death. DeeDee also placed a picture of the family in the casket with her. She wanted to make sure that Kiki remembered them so she would know who to look for when they were all up in heaven.

Mr. Brown, the funeral director did all he could to try to make James look like himself, but it was almost impossible. Desiree decided to keep his casket closed so everyone would remember how handsome he once was. As Desiree and the children were passing by the bodies, to pay their final respects, Dre paused in front of his father's casket. He placed his hand upon it and tearfully whispered,

"Don't you worry Pops…I made you a promise and I'm a man of my word. I got your back…cause you always had mine. I…love…you."

Desiree held up pretty well at the church in spite of her loss. She bent down and kissed James' casket, then little Kiki's face. Dre and his uncle Terry, his mother's younger brother, had to pull her away as she broke down. "My baby! …Oh God…why'd you take my baby," she cried, reaching for the casket.

At the cemetery, James received a 21-gun salute. He served 15 years in the marines before he was wounded in Vietnam. Each time the color guard's rifles cracked like thunder, DeeDee jumped and squealed. The bodies were laid to rest side by side next to James' parents. There were so many beautiful flowers that it took four station wagons to carry them. They were all aligned next to their graves. As they slowly lowered the caskets into the cold dark grave, Desiree collapsed to the ground.

5, 4, 3, 2, 1…HAPPY NEW YEAR!

Nineteen hundred and Seventy-Seven starts a new year of new beginnings. It's been less than two months since the deaths of James and Kiki. The family was trying desperately to pick up the pieces and pull together as one. Christmas was a very difficult time for everyone. No one wanted to put up a tree or decorate the house. James would always go and pick out the perfect tree for the family and bring it home all proud. No one could find the strength to replace his tradition. There were no mouth watering smells of honey baked ham, sweet potato pies, or homemade yeast rolls coming out of the kitchen this year. Instead, they ordered pizza and popped corn.

DeeDee and Dre have been extremely helpful around the house. DeeDee, although only twelve, makes sure that dinner is ready and on the table by the time her mother gets home from work. Desiree doesn't even have to remind Dre to cut the grass or wash the car on Saturday, as she always had to do before. In fact, Dre began cutting several neighbors lawns in order to get his own extra money so he wouldn't have to burden his mother for his spending change. DeeDee babysits for her extra money and Shannon gets her little candy money by helping her brother and sister with their chores. When James died, he had no life insurance; therefore, Desiree was left with all of the burial expenses for the funeral as well as the normal family expenses. Although the couple had a little "nest egg" in the bank, it long since had been used up. Despite Desiree making a decent living, it just wasn't enough to keep up with the once two income family budget.

Desiree's problems do not end there. Two weeks after the funeral, she found out that she was pregnant. She and James were not planning to have another baby in fact he was considering a vasectomy. Desiree had not told the children of her pregnancy because she had terrible mixed emotions about it. Financially, she was already over her head, and emotionally, she was torn between feelings as though life was hard enough raising three children without the love and support of her husband. She knew that if she were to have this baby her life would be more complex and stressful. Yet, Desiree could not help but feel as though her pregnancy was simply a gift from God. Maybe He was just giving her back the baby she'd lost. Desiree had confided her secret with her mother, Eva. The two were very close. Eva, a 62-year-old retired nurse, had been living with her daughter and her family since the death of Desiree's father in 1970. Desiree convinced her mother to sell her house and move closer to the family so they could look after her. Even though Eva's breast cancer had been in remission for over ten years, she was beginning to show some signs of Alzheimer's disease.

Eva and her late husband, Jesse owned a small house near Austin, Texas, and with her two children, Desiree and son Terry both living in Miami she would be all alone with no one close to care for her in case of an emergency. Eva has been very supportive of her daughter, but the decision about her pregnancy was totally up to her. Eva did tell her that having another child at this time was not a good idea, but whatever she decided she would do everything she could to help her.

Desiree was entering into her fourth month when she finally decided to abort her pregnancy. Luckily for her she had not yet begun to show so she was still able to keep her pregnancy a secret. She never knew just how expensive the procedure was. It had only been a few years since the Supreme Court decision, "Roe vs. Wade" made abortion legal, and therefore the clinics that offered late term abortions in her area were limited and very expensive. A friend of hers told her about a Haitian woman who helped women terminate their pregnancies. She was a little skeptical about going to someone other than a certified doctor, but her friend said she knew of other women who had gone to her so she convinced Desiree that it was safe.

It was already after 6pm, and Dre was beginning to worry about his mother who was normally home by 4 o'clock sharp every day. Nana knew where her daughter had gone. Today was the day she had to go and take care of her "situation."

Desiree finally came home around 7:45pm that evening. She headed straight upstairs to her room, not even noticing Dre in the living room.

"Hey ma"

"Oh...hey baby ...where's everybody?" she said leaning against the stair well for support. She was very weak and feeling woozy from the anesthesia.

"Nana and the girls went to the movies. She said you would be tired when you got home so she was getting them out of the house so they wouldn't bother you. Ma...are you alright?" he said noticing her hunching over.

"Yeah…baby I'm fine; momma's just a little tired that's all."

"Nana made some lasagna…want some?"

"Yeah…just a little bit though, I'm not very hungry but I'd better put something on my stomach."

"Okay, let me wash my hands then I'll bring it up to you."

"Thank you baby…you know how to take care of your momma don't you? What would I do with you?" she said as she disappeared slowly up the stairs.

"I don't know ma, but you're stuck with me." As he began fixing his mother's plate he heard a familiar knock at the door. He knew it was one of his boys Domino or T.J. They had a certain code knock so they would know it was one of them. Dre opened the door.

"What's up nigga," said Domino, the wildest of the bunch, as he entered.

"Shhh, chill man…my mother is upstairs sick." Domino put his hand over his mouth and apologized. He and Dre had been best friends since the first grade. When Dre and his family lived in the projects Domino and T.J. lived next door from them. Since they moved out and bought a house about six years ago the boys have still remained close. Every weekend they got together and played ball in the hood. The three of them together were unstoppable. They each played on their Jr. Varsity squads at different middle schools. Domino, whose real name is Robert Foster, is biracial, mixed half-black and half-white. His mother was white and she grew up in the same projects that they live in today. She had Domino when she was only thirteen years old pregnant by a hardhead boy that's been in prison for the past eight years.

Violence is all Domino knows. He lives in a rough part of town, attends a school with a gang problem, and watched his father beat up his mother for years. Last year his older brother was found dead in the trunk of a car, killed by some small-time drug dealers in the neighborhood. They accused him of stealing their product that they had hidden away, but in actuality, Domino had stolen the drugs. Domino harbors a lot of guilt and hate inside over his brother's death. He is constantly getting in trouble in school or with the police. If he was not fighting or gangbanging, he was being caught stealing cars or robbing liquor stores. Desiree didn't want Dre hanging around with him anymore because she was afraid Domino would get her son into trouble or killed.

T.J. finally came into the house. He had been outside talking to DeeDee. Her and her grandmother had just returned home from the movies. They've had a crush on each other since last summer but Dre didn't approve.

"Hey man, I done 'told you about my sister man," said Dre. T.J looked at him in confusion. "What?"

"Nigga, you know what! You ain't shit and you know it. You better leave her alone man, I don't want to have to mess you up," said Dre with a grin, but he was serious and T.J. knew it.

"Man…you be trippin." "I didn't say that when you wanted to get with my cousin Rita, did I?" Dre had a thing for Spanish girls. T.J. was originally from Puerto Rico. He and his family moved to Miami when he was two. He was an All-American center at Roosevelt Middle school and was sure to get a scholarship. At age 14, T.J., short for Torez Jaramillo, already stood 6'3" and was hounded by high school recruiters who wanted him for next year. All three of the boys had dreams of getting recruited by a major university and going to the pros. This is why every weekend, in addition to practicing all week in school, the boys played from sun up to sun down.

"Hurry up man, so we can go kick some ass. We owe them punk-ass niggas from last week," said Domino.

"Domino, watch your mouth man, my grandmother is coming in the front door. Man...you need to respect my mother's house," Dre reminded Domino.

"Anyway, I'm not sure if I should leave because my mother ain't feeling good and she might need me for something."

"Man I swear you ain't nothin' but a momma's boy. We ain't gonna be gone long, you know they cut the lights out on the courts at 11 on weekdays," said a frustrated Domino. Dre thought to himself for a minute.

"Well...my grandmother is home now, she'll keep an eye on her...man...I do want to go hoop dough. All right wait a minute...let me take her plate upstairs right quick and tell my grandmother where I'm going," said Dre trying to rush. When Dre got upstairs his mother was already asleep. Pictures of his father and Kiki sat neatly on her nightstand facing her pillow. She never went to sleep without telling her husband about her day, how she missed him, how much she loved him, and to give their little girl a kiss for her. After she said her prayers she would kiss their pictures and try to dream life back into them. Dre sat the tray of food on her nightstand, kissed his mother gently on the forehead, and darted downstairs.

The night couldn't have been better. The trio won three out of four games and they were still hyped. All the way home they discussed play-by-play highlights, of each other's spectacular shots, and moves. T.J. blocked six shots tonight, and Dre, a high percentage outside shooter couldn't miss. Dre has led the county in scoring for two years now. Domino is so quick with his hands; his position is at point where he takes control. In addition, of course, the night wouldn't be complete without Domino getting into a fight.

As they walked down Madison Ave. heading to Dre's house and laughing about the scuffle, fire trucks and ambulances hurried pass them. The boys assumed that because it was Friday night in the hood, someone had either been shot, stabbed, robbed, or raped. But when the vehicles turned down Dre's street they took off running to see what was happening.

"Maybe it's just an accident or something," yelled T.J., partly out of breath.
"Come on T.J., hurry up," shouted Dre.
"I know man…T.J. runs like a little bitch," laughed Domino.
"Man…Fuck you man, I'm tired," replied T.J.

"Oh shit," screamed Dre. Just then he realized the fire trucks had stopped at his house. Neighbors were all outside on their front porches and standing on their lawns trying to find out what was happening. As Dre pushed himself through the crowd, a tall white officer grabbed him. The crowd looked on because they knew he lived there. "Let me go, I live here!" Dre was desperately searching for his grandmother, his mother, sisters, or somebody. Suddenly appearing from out of the house his Uncle Terry came holding DeeDee, who appeared to be crying. Right then he knew something was terribly wrong. His heart was racing and tears were beginning to fill his eyes. When his uncle saw him, he yelled for the officer to let him threw. Dre raced up the stairs and onto the crowded porch.

"What's going on man?" cried Dre as he reached his uncle. DeeDee never looked up. She was crying uncontrollably.

Terry looked at his nephew with tears in his eyes, "It's your mother…she's gone Dre."

Dre slowly backed away, shaking his head.
"What do you mean…my moth…what the fuck you talking about man," Dre yelled, as he tore through the doorway and ran up the stairs, pushing through the paramedics and more police. "Ma…Ma," he yelled as he finally reached her bedroom door. There were so many people crowded in the room he couldn't see inside. He shoved his way through the crowd, yelling for his mother, hoping she would answer back. When he finally made it to her bed, he saw his grandmother hunched over her crying. She looked as if she were sleeping, just as he had left her.

"No…momma…no," he screamed as he fell on the edge of her bed. His grandmother looked up and reached for him but he pulled away.

"She's gone baby…your momma's gone," she said tearfully. He just stood there still shaking his head in disbelief.

"No she's not grandma...she's just sleeping...she's real tired that's all. Tell them mom," he said as he grabbed his mother's arm trying to lift her up. "Wake up ma...stop playing now...you're scaring grandma...ma please wake up!"

One of the paramedics grabbed him trying to stop him from pulling on his lifeless mother.

"Come on son, she's gone...we got to take her now," said a deep and unfamiliar voice. It was the coroner. He was a very large dark man, wearing a white jacket and light blue pants. Dre wasn't going for that. He snatched away from the heavyset man and continued to reach for his mother. It took three police to pull the screaming boy out of the room. As they lifted Desiree's blood soaked body from the bed, the pictures of her husband and daughter fell to the floor. When her mother found her, she was apparently cradling them in her arms.

AN UNWELCOMED SURPRISE

The procession of cars that headed towards the cemetery seemed to be never-ending. Leading the line was a gray hearse carrying the body of Desiree. After her was a white station wagon filled with flowers from friends and relatives. Her grieving mother and children followed in a black limousine. It seemed like an eternity before the slow moving line of cars reached Desiree's final resting place. The rain began to pour as mourners gathered around the site. As Dre sat next to his grandmother he glanced at the headstones of his father and sister. He and his mother had just recently visited the graves just two weeks before. Dre noticed the flowers they left behind barely clinging to life. His heart was heavy. He felt as though he had failed his family and broken his promise to his father. He believed that if he would have worked harder then maybe things would have been easier for his mother and she would have kept the baby. He also believed that if he had not gone to play ball, and watched over her when he knew she was sick then she would not have bled to death. "What's going to become of him and his sisters now," he thought, as everyone bowed their heads in prayer. Within the silence, Dre heard his grandmother whisper,

"...Oh my dear God!" He lifted his head and looked at her. She was staring at a tall broad man holding a single yellow rose. Those were Desiree's favorite. "But who was he," Dre thought to himself.

"What the hell is he doing here," said his Uncle Terry. The stranger moved towards the casket and placed the rose upon it. He appeared to be crying but it was hard to tell because he had been standing in the rain. Dre thought that maybe he was a friend of his mother's from work or something, but that did not explain his grandmother and uncle's reactions. Finally he had to ask,

"Yo, Uncle Terry, who's that dude over there?" Terry turned the boy around as they began to walk away from the site,

"Nobody, come on let's go," he said in an angry voice.

Later on at the house many family members and friends came over with food and offered their condolences. Dre sat on the porch with his grandmother in her swing chair. She was still very upset about Desiree. She too felt a little responsible for her daughter's death because she was the only one that Desiree confided in. She wished she would have talked her out of the abortion, and convinced her that she would be there to help her with the baby. Dre tried to comfort her as best as he could because the last thing he wanted was for her to make herself sick. Dre felt now more than ever before that he had to step forward and take control of his family. Financially, they were in trouble. Desiree's life insurance was cancelled for non-payment so there was no money for the children. Fortunately the church was able to raise enough money for the funeral expenses and then some but it wouldn't last. The only money his grandmother had coming in was a little disability and his grandfather's social security. This was hardly enough to pay the $800.00 mortgage payment or the car payment. The children would probably receive some sort of check from their parents' social security as well as some assistance from the state, but they were still headed for a struggle. Never the less, Dre was determined to do everything he could to save his family.

Mr. Fredrick offered Dre a little part-time job working in his grocery store after school. Since Dre was only thirteen, he could not legally work, so he had to be paid under the table. This was actually to Mr. Frederick's advantage because now he could pay him a lot less and save money.

It has been almost three weeks since Desiree passed. Eva is coping with the loss of her daughter slowly but surely. She keeps herself busy with trying to raise her three grandchildren the best way she can. Every Sunday, she makes sure they're in Sunday school at 7:30 sharp. The children have always had a strong religious foundation, but she knew she needed the Lord's help with keeping them on the right track. DeeDee and Dre were honor roll students. Academics have never been a problem in the Snipes household, because the children knew their parents did not play, and weren't tolerating bad grades. Desiree always instilled in her children the importance of a good education. Dre hoped to play ball at Duke University, go to the pros, and then continue his education in law. DeeDee was interested in a criminal justice major. She wanted to be a secret agent for the government.

Every day after school Dre had practice until 6pm, which became a problem, because Mr. Frederick needed him earlier for deliveries. He normally got home in the evening around 11pm, exhausted from his day, but he still had his studies. It was usually after 1:30 in the morning that he was able to get in bed, only to be up again at 4:30am. He obtained another job delivering the morning paper. The weekends were just as hectic for the young boy. He worked at the drugstore from 8:30am until 7pm. Afterwards he would come home and cut his grass, and two of the neighbor's yards which normally took him well into the night to complete. Between school, basketball practices, games and three jobs, Dre had little time for himself. He was definitely wearing himself thin and his grandmother knew it. She insisted that he quit working and put everything in God's hands, and believe that He will provide. All of his money usually went towards a light bill here, a car payment there, or groceries. The phone and cable had long since been disconnected, and the mortgage payment was past due. There just wasn't enough money and this made Dre frustrated. Although he was just a young boy, he had the weight of the world on his tiny shoulders.

One evening while Dre was in his room studying, he heard voices arguing downstairs. He immediately went to the top of the stairs and there he saw his uncle and the stranger from the cemetery.

"I told you to keep your ass away from here Sterling! Desiree wanted you out of her life and her sons," yelled Uncle Terry.

"He's my son too damn it! My son! When I got home from prison, I didn't know where to find them. You and your mother wasn't no fucking help, ya'll never wanted us together anyway," said the tall man as he became louder with frustration.

"No one wanted you around because you were no damn good...nothing but trouble. You caused my sister a lot of grief. The best thing she ever did was to leave you and marry James.

"Listen Terry, this doesn't even concern you. I'm Dre's father and it's time he knew me."

Dre could not believe his ears. He always knew James wasn't his real father but he never imagined actually getting to meet his biological father. He didn't know whether to be happy or pissed off. Why did he wait so long to come find him, and where has he been? Dre slowly walked to the top of the stairs towards his uncle and the man claiming to be his father. By this time all of the noise had awakened Eva.

"Terry is that you down there, what's going on?" she asked as she stood on top of the stairs wearing her robe and rubbing her eyes trying to focus. "Who are you down there talking to?" she asked.

"Momma...go back to bed, it's alright." Terry walked to the edge of the stairs and looked up at his mother. He didn't want her to get upset about Sterling being there. It was then that he also noticed Dre standing there. "Dre go to bed, it's late." Dre wasn't budging. There was no way he was leaving without answers.

"Grandma…this man said he was my father…is that true?" Dre walked down the stairs and up to the stranger. Eva follows behind him. Dre looked him up and down checking out his expensive clothes and jewelry. Once she got her eyes focused enough to see the tall figure standing in her living room she yelled out.

"Why are you coming around here trying to bring trouble into my boys' life?" Dre realized this man was not welcomed around here but why? Why did his mother leave him and marry James? Why did everybody hate him so much? Eva began threatening to call the police if he didn't leave. Sterling insisted he wasn't there to start any trouble, he only wanted a minute with his son, and he was not leaving until Dre heard his side of the story. Dre went upstairs and tried to calm his grandmother down. He assured her that everything would be fine and he wouldn't talk long. He begged her to allow him to meet his father. Eva hesitated because she knew Desiree would not want for Dre to be in contact with his no-good father, but she soon agree only if Terry was there to hear everything that was said. She wanted to make sure that Sterling wasn't going to try to poison his mind with lies about his mother.

The three went outside on the porch to talk. At first, Sterling seemed to be lost for words. He appeared to be very nervous, unlike the man who just bucked up to his uncle. He cleared his throat, cracked his big knuckles, ironically just as Dre did when he was nervous, and slowly began to speak.

"I don't really know where to begin. I guess my name is a good place to start," he nervously chuckled. "I'm Sterling Lanier...your father. I want you to know I loved your mother...hell I still do, but I didn't do right by her...and she left me. I now when I leave your grandmother and uncle will tell you that I am a monster, and I'm no good...well that was true in the past. I had a drug problem a long time ago, but I'm straight now though."

"Is that why my mother left you?" asked Dre as he nervously picked leaves from the bush beside him and threw them down.

"Yeah...that and because I ran around with some dangerous people and she thought I was putting the two of you in danger, but I would have never let anything happen to ya'll and she knew that. Dre, you were just a tiny baby when she took you away from me, so you don't remember how much I loved you, and how proud I was to be a father," Sterling said as he fought back the tears. Dre looked at his pitiful looking father. He wanted to embrace him and feel compassion towards him, but he couldn't overlook his feelings of anger.

"Well if you loved me so much, then where have you been, and why has it taken you so long to find me?" he said enraged. Sensing his son's frustrations, Sterling humbly tried to account for his absence.

"Son, I tried for a long time...but I didn't know where to find you. I spent some time in prison...and by the time I got out and found your mother she had already married someone else, and had another child. She told me to stay out of her life...that she was happy, and it would be best for you if I stayed away."

"So you just forgot about me huh?" said Dre sarcastically.

"Hell no...I never stopped wondering how you were and if you were alright. Every year I sent birthday cards to your grandmother's house in Texas, because that's the only address I had, hoping that I would hear from your mother...but she never called. I guess you never got them, huh?"

"I never got anything from you. Look man, it's getting late and I promised my grandmother that I wouldn't be long. What is it that you want from me now?" Sterling walked closer to his son. He desperately searched for the right words to say. He quickly flashed back to the time with he was twenty years old, and his father, who had also abandoned his mother, and left her alone with four young children suddenly appeared at his front door after eleven years asking for money. He remembered the many days when they had no food and had to go to bed hungry, and how much he hated his father for not caring. There was nothing his father could say to him that day, and he feared Dre had those same feelings for him.

"I...want to be a father to you. I want us to get to know each other...I want to help you...be there for you."

"Be a father?" said Terry laughingly, who up until then had been only silently monitoring the conversation. Dre looked at Sterling and shook his head.

"As far as I'm concerned, my father, James Snipes is dead. He's the only father I had. He's the one that's been there for me and my mom...taught me how to play ball...made sure we had food and a roof over our heads. No...you can't be anything to me. I don't need you now. You could have found me if you really wanted to.

"Dre, I'm here now. Let me make up for it, support you," he said desperately trying to reach his son. "How are you guys making it anyway? Who's paying the bills? I have lots of money Dre, I can help."

"Oh yeah...well you look like a pimp or something to me. "What's up?" Sterling paused before he answered him. He wanted to be as truthful with his son as he possibly could. Terry looked at him, anxiously waiting to see what he would say because he knew the truth.

"Okay look…I don't stand on corners and hustle or nothing like that. I'm more of a investor…you know…on the business aspect of things."

Dre chuckled, "Yeah right, just what I thought a drug dealer…pimp…same thing. Now I see what my family is talking about…you are bad news, and I am definitely better off without you. We might not have much right now…but we do love each other. Right now I have three jobs, and I'm taking care of my family like my father would have wanted me to," he said proudly. "I'm being a man…something you really don't know about, "Dre said as he turned around to walk back in the house. Those words cut Sterling deep. He grabbed the screen door before it could close behind his son. He reached inside his coat pocket, pulled out an envelope, and gave it to Dre. Dre slowly opened it and inside were several $100 bills.

"There's $2000 dollars in there…I want you to have it. I can give you more if you need it." Dre looked down at the money. It was more than he had ever seen at one time before. Then he stared straight into Sterling's eyes, "Keep your dirty money," he said, as he handed Sterling back the envelope. Sterling stood back and gazed at what he thought to be a little boy, he now realized was a bigger man than he was. For Sterling knew he was easily drawn into the game when he was just about Dre's age. If someone would have offered him money, he would not have had to think twice. He respected his son for standing his ground. He knew guys in the streets that would not stand up to him as he did. Sterling was impressed.

"Okay...man I respect that. I am proud of you, and I see James did a good job of raising you. I wish I could shake his hand and thank him personally. Here is my number...please...call me if you need anything," he said as he placed it in Dre's hand, not giving him a chance to reject it. "Maybe we can get together and play some ball or something," he said, still refusing to stop trying to reach him. Without saying a word, Dre turned and walked away.

Over the next few months life became very
hectic for the Snipes family. Their house went into
foreclosure, the car was repossessed, and Eva's health
was beginning to deteriorate. The family was forced to
move back into public housing and a social worker was
assigned to them. There had been reports to HRS that
Dre was forced to work extremely long hours and there
was not adequate supervision for the children.

Life in the projects was very different from the
way the children were used to living. They had gone
from a five bedroom, two-story house with a pool in
Coconut Grove, a very prestigious area of Miami, to a
two bedroom, roach infested unit that sat in the midst of
poverty, destruction, and violence. Each night, directly
beneath their doorstep there were murders and drug
deals. There were heroin addicts lying on their stairs,
begging for money from anyone who passed by. Other
than going to and from school, Eva didn't allow the girls
outside. She was too afraid that someone would grab
them, or worst try to give them drugs. At anytime a crap
game could turn deadly. Gang graffiti blanketed the
building in which they were now forced to call home.

DeeDee and Shannon were no longer able to
attend the private Christian academy they had been
enrolled in for years. Instead, they were subjected to
lower educational systems, gang and racial tension, and
insufficient teachings. However, since Dre was in a
public middle school, he was able to remain there for his
final year. Surprisingly in spite of their economic
situation, the family generally remained bright and

optimistic simply because they knew how it was to lose so much in so little time that they were just grateful still to have each other.

One evening the social worker came to the house unexpectedly, but this time she did not come alone. Her name was Evelyn Goldstein, and with her came another woman that introduced herself as Mrs. Hutchinson, her immediate supervisor, in charge of Child Protective Services. Mrs. Goldstein had already visited the house twice before. She never said much but she always did a lot of writing. She was a fairly large woman with long brown hair that she normally wore tied up in a bun. She wore bifocals that sat on the edge of her nose and brought attention to her mustache. Mrs. Hutchinson, slightly younger and much more attractive stood intimidatingly in the living room. She wore a neatly tailored tan suit with an eggshell white blouse. She reached within her briefcase and pulled out a report created by Mrs. Goldstein's that included her evaluation of the family. She went on to inform Eva that the report stated she was not physically, nor financially able to care for her minor grandchildren. She knew of Eva's failing mental condition as well as her cancer, and insisted the children needed another adult to look after them.

Eva slowly sat done on the couch in disbelief. Tears began to fill her matured eyes. They were trying to take her babies from her and she could do nothing to stop them. DeeDee ran towards her grandmother and held on for dear life.

"Don't you worry baby, Nana ain't gone let the devil come in here and take ya'll away from me. I know…cause God done already showed me dat." "So we just gone pray and keep on praying." Eva said, as she slowly rose to her feet and looked at the two women. "Don't you think these children have gone through enough?"

"Ma'am, I realize what they've gone through over the past year, and believe me I do sympathize with them. We are only trying to do what is best for them so they will not have to endure anymore suffering. I know you love your grandchildren Mrs. Horne, but I'm just doing my job," explained Mrs. Hutchinson as she packed up her briefcase and headed for the door. "I'm going to need a list of any relatives that are willing and financially able to care for the minor children. Unfortunately…there is a chance they may have to be separated unless someone can afford to take on the responsibility of all three." She placed her card on the coffee table and both of the ladies walked out of the front door.

The next few days were excruciating. Eva had very little to say to anyone. She spent most of her time cleaning and singing spiritual hymns. It was apparent that she was placing everything in God's hands. Her faith in the Lord was very strong, but Dre knew it was going to take a little more than that. There was no family, at least no one willing to take all three of them. There was his father's half-sister, aunt Gladys, that lived in Detroit, Michigan, but she already had four children of her own. Their paternal grandmother Alice was willing to take DeeDee and Shannon, but of course not Dre. She never really accepted him as her grandson. The only other relative was Uncle Terry. Terry was a 34-year-old program director for a local television station in Miami. He had never been married, nor had he any children of his own, but he was very close with his nieces and nephew. Financially, he was able to help care for the children, and was willing to do everything he could to help.

Until the family came up with a better solution, Terry was able to convince Child Protective Services that he could adequately provide for the children. He assured them that he would move in the apartment with the children and take over as guardian. Although Terry had no real intentions of moving in with them because he already lived with his girlfriend, Yolanda, but it was enough to get social services off their backs, at least until they came up with a better plan.

Unfortunately for Dre, because of his work schedule, he had to sit out when the new basketball season began. This hurt the young man deeply. Basketball was his life, his dream, and it looked as if those hopes for a scholarship, or the pros' were fading. Even thought he was receiving more help from his uncle, he still had a lot of pressure on him. While most boys his age were outside hanging out, chasing girls, or just doing typical boy things, fourteen-year-old Dre was wearing the shoes of a man. Eva's doctor bills and medications were beginning to escalate. Because of the sudden death of her daughter, and worrying about her grandchildren, her health was deteriorating rapidly. She was fading away before Dre's eyes and he felt so helpless. Her weary eyes no longer held the spirit, and life that they once possessed. Depression was taking over her soul, and most of the time she just sat upstairs in her room gazing blankly out of the window for hours, seldom responding to the children at all. She would often believe she was having conversations with her dead daughter. She needed special attention fast. This disturbed Dre deeply. He was too young to really understand that there was no a whole lot that he could do for his grandmother. He believed if they had more money, that she could get the proper help and get better. He hated leaving her alone everyday but there was no one that could care for her while they were in school. He felt his family slipping through his fingers, and once again, the burden of his family intensified.

"Nervous," asked DeeDee, as she watched Dre running back and forth, up and down the stairs. Tonight was the state finals championship game, Dre had a few college scouts coming to see him, and he was only a sophomore. Of course he was nervous but he had to play macho. After having to sit out his freshman year, he worried about being able to jump back into a starting position on the team, but because he was such a skilled player, he had no problem.

"DeeDee...you seen my other shoe," he asked, as he looked beneath the couch. "Ask Nana, I think she washed them for you this morning, and hurry up so them stupid friends of yours will stop blowing that loud horn!"

"Wait, I'm coming," he shouted out of the door. "And stop blowing the horn, my grandmother is resting!" Dre finally found his things for the game and in a mad dash he darted out of the door and jumped into the backseat of TJ's mother's beat up car.

"Damn nigga, what wuz you doin', jackin' off," laughed T.J.

"Yeah, smell my hand," joked Dre.

"Hey man, I know you're ready to flex in front of those scouts tonight," said Domino. "What you goin'hit, a triple double?"

"You know it, my nigga!" Dre and T.J. were on the same team. This was T.J.'s last year. He too had scouts interested in him, but not like Dre. There were scouts from Syracuse, North Carolina, and Georgetown in town just for him. He was number one in the state in scoring and rebounding. Domino on the other hand got into some major trouble and had been a suspect in a murder investigation, so he could not play this season.

"Damn D., I sure wish you were playing against us tonight. I would sure look good showing off to you," laughed Dre.

"Hey ya'll goin' have to find another ride home man, cause I've got some plans after the game," said T.J.

"That's cool, but them plans better not include my sister nigga," Dre said with a serious voice. Dre knew T.J. had a crush on DeeDee and she liked him too, but Dre didn't like the idea of his friend messing with his little sister.

"Man, DeeDee be looking fine in that little cheerleading outfit. What ya'll been feeding that filly Dre," joked Domino, as he gave T.J. a high five. Dre didn't think those comments about his sister were funny at all.

"I hope I don't have to knock your ass out before the game man."

"Man chill, I'm just trying to get you hyped for the game... (*long pause*)...but she is getting thick though," TJ whispered. The trio laughed as they headed for Park Springs High.

The score was tied 73 all, with 15 seconds left on the clock. Dre, as expected, had been shooting Central's eyes out all night long. He had already scored 37 points, 12 rebounds, and 11 assists, and the triple double that he'd promised his boys. This game had been tight all night and the crowd was out of control. His grandmother and Uncle Terry were there as always cheering him on. It was Central's ball, the seconds were quickly dwindling down, but they missed the shot! With only seconds left, Park Springs headed down the court. Dre got the ball and drove inside for a layup or foul, it didn't matter. As he released the ball he was knocked off his feet.

"Buzz!" It went in! Park Springs had taken the title. The crowd roared and rushed the floor. The coaching staff noticed Dre still lying on the court and he appeared to be in pain.

"Coach, it's my knee! Oh God...my knee," he cried in anguish. As his teammates carried him to the bench Uncle Terry hurried toward him with concern. The scouts also looked on in despair.

"Let's get him in the back quick! Get everyone back now! Where is that damn stretcher? Move it, move it," screamed coach Lynch. The coaches rushed him in the locker room to get a better look. Things did not look good for Dre. The team doctor couldn't determine how bad it was without x-rays. Dre was in a lot of pain and he was terrified about his knee. He saw the scout from Georgetown talking to his coach in the office.

"Why tonight," he thought to himself. Basketball was going to be his family's ticket out of the projects. There was no way the three of them were going to be able to go to college without scholarships. Howard Faup, the scout from Georgetown came over to where Dre was lying.

"Impressive game champ," he said. Don't worry about that knee hopefully it's not serious. We'd love to have you in Georgetown in a couple of years," he assured Dre. He shook his hand and walked out of the locker room with the team doctor. Dre knew the doctor was not saying anything promising.

The next day Dre's room was filled with balloons and flowers sent by friends and teachers from school. Dre was the fallen hero that night, but he couldn't celebrate with the others. His knee was worst than they thought. He tore his ACL and would need several surgeries over the next few years which meant his dreams of playing college or professional basketball were shattered. Dre was crushed…All of his life he practiced day in and day out for his scholarship. He ate and slept basketball. True enough he also planned to obtain a law degree as well. His parents were very strict about education and his career was priority. Now without a scholarship, how would he pay for college?

The next few months were very depressing for him. He was unsure as to what his next move should be. Since his basketball hopes were over he had to concentrate more on his grades and obtaining an academic scholarship. Because of his busy schedule the trio hardly spent time together. Sometimes weeks would pass before they would see each other. Dre didn't have much time to be a typical teenager, hanging out at malls, and going on dates like most kids his age. Between school and his full-time job, he barely had time to get proper rest. Soon Dre would be fifteen, but still too young to get a real job, so he would have to continue to be overworked and underpaid by Old Man Frederick.

Dre enjoyed his walks home from work. Sometimes he would cut through the woods and go the long way home just to avoid passing the park where he knew his friends would be playing ball. He hated to see them playing because he wanted to play so bad. One evening Mr. Frederick's wife took ill and had to be rushed to the hospital so he closed early. Dre was not happy that she was sick, but he was glad to be going home before dark for a change. Just as he was about to come to the opening out of the woods he noticed a wooden crate lying on the ground. This would be perfect for Shannon's new rabbit he thought. As he knelt down to pick it up he noticed a pile of leaves. Curious as to what someone might be trying to hide under there, he started digging through the shallow brush.

"Oh shit," he said as he uncovered a mayonnaise jar filled with what appeared to be joints. At first he was terrified because he knew someone had placed them there and they would soon be back for them. He neatly put the jar back under the pile of leaves and began to walk away. As he continued to walk out of the woods he could think of nothing else. There had to be over two hundred joints in that jar, or maybe more, he thought to himself. As he entered his house DeeDee erupted,

"What are you doing here so early? Did you get fired or something," asked DeeDee, as she cleaned the kitchen.

"Mind your business sometime. You're just mad because Nana said I don't have to wash dishes," teased Dre. He enjoyed teasing his sisters, and they hated it.

"Shut up, big head," shouted DeeDee, as she flung soapy water at him.

"Stop ole' crazy girl," he shouted.

"Shhhh," said DeeDee. Nana isn't feeling too good tonight. She needed to get her medicine last week but she didn't have enough money so she's been in a lot of pain." Dre hated to see her suffering. She sacrificed so much for them, but it was taking a toll on her health. He didn't have any money and he wasn't getting paid until next Friday. Their uncle was always crying broke because he had to support his family and help support them. Dre went upstairs to check on his grandmother.

She was lying on the bed in a cold sweat. Her pressure had gone up so bad that she couldn't even lift her head from the pillow. Dre was crushed. He could not just let her lay there in pain like that. He knew what he needed to do. He headed out the door and back into the woods in search of the buried treasure that he'd left behind.

As he lay in bed that night and stared at the jar, he wondered if he should go and place it back once again. He was always the one telling his friends about how wrong it was for someone to sell drugs. He knew what he was thinking about doing was bad but he had nowhere else to turn. Life was getting harder and harder for the family, and his grandmother's health was weakening every day. She was the entire mother he had left and he wasn't about to just let her slip away like his parents did.

Dre didn't know the first thing about selling drugs. He had often seen guys standing on the street corners and running up to cars, but he didn't know exactly what went on next. He wasn't even sure how much he should sell the joints for. He realized that if he was going to do this, he needed help.

Although Dre stayed up half the night planning his strategy, he was up and out of the house before 8am. Because it was Saturday, he knew T.J. and Domino would still be in the bed, but he didn't care. First he headed to T.J.'s house because he wanted to discuss it with him. T.J. was very mature for his age and he knew he could give him good advice on what he should do. He already knew that his delinquent friend Domino would be down for anything illegal. He wasn't even sure whether or not he should tell Domino. He had a big mouth and he liked to brag about his business all the time. Dre definitely did not want to be known as the neighborhood drug dealer. He just wanted to get rid of the jar, make a little cash so his grandmother could get her medicine, and wash his hands of it.

"Man, where did you get that?" asked T.J., as he wiped the sleep from his eyes snatching the jar from Dre. Dre told his friend the whole story of how he found the drugs. T.J. reminded Dre that he could get himself hurt if the rightful owner of the stash found out who had his drugs.

"Don't you think I know this man? What if this is "Wicked's" shit? You know he don't play when it comes to his money man. I could find my ass in a trunk rotting somewhere." T.J. told him that he would help him do whatever he needed him to, but he didn't know anymore about selling weed than Dre did. He agreed that telling Domino might be a mistake, but he was the only one who would know the best way of getting rid of the stuff.

"Whew shit! It's on my nigga," Domino celebrated as he grabbed the jar from Dre opening the lid and smelling inside to get a closer look. "This is some good shit too man."

"How do you know," asked Dre.

"The smell," said Domino. Domino could have told Dre anything at this point and he would have believed him. "So you the man now huh," joked Domino.

"Hell no, nor am I trying to be. You know how I feel about this D. After this is gone, that's it. I am not trying to get locked up."

"Look Dre, check this out," said Domino. "Your green ass don't know the first thing about the streets, but I do. Let me get rid of this for you, and you stay in the background," he suggested. Domino thought he came up with that plan, but little did he know that was Dre's plan all along. Dre wasn't planning to use his friend, but he knew that this would be up Domino's alley. This way he could volunteer, instead of Dre telling him to. Dre already knew that Domino would probably keep the majority of the money for himself, but he didn't care as long as he got enough to get his grandmother's medicine.

Dre could hardly believe it. The next day Domino showed up at his house with $175 for him.

"Get the fuck out of here," said Dre in amazement. He couldn't believe how fast Domino was able to make that money. So they would bring any attention to themselves, Domino went to an area in Ft. Lauderdale and got rid of the weed. He was very familiar with that part of town because his grandparents had lived there ever since he was a baby, so he knew everyone. Domino told Dre that he only kept a hundred for himself so he could have enough to get what he needed for his grandmother.

It made him feel good to see her eyes light up when he showed her the money.

"Lord Jesus boy, where did you get this money child?" she asked as he put it in her hands. I hope you ain't out there doing nothing you ain't suppose to."

"No ma'am, I'm not. Is it enough for your medicine Nana?"

"More than enough, enough for three prescriptions," she smiled.

"Good, I'll go down to the drug store and get your medicine for three months so you don't have to worry about it for a while," he said as he bent down and kissed her cheek. Dre felt like the man of the house for the first time in a long time. He was there when his family really needed him, and he was proud.

A NECESSARY EVIL

The fallen dead leaves had completely covered the stone markers of the Snipes family. Dre, as he has for the last couple of years, made his monthly visit. The cemetery was not far from his church so he usually went after services. He wiped the leaves to reveal the names as he sat between the two graves. The bouquet of yellow roses that he had left before had long since dried up. He felt a sense of peace each time he went to his parent's graves. Sometimes he just sat and reminisced about the good times they used to have and the love the family shared. He missed them so much and he knew it would be a long time before he would get over their deaths.

Today he needed to talk to them about what he had done. He had already asked God for forgiveness in church that morning, but he felt as if he must apologize to his mother and father. Dre never wanted to disappoint them in life and he felt the same way in their deaths. He believed they were angels in heaven watching over him and his sisters, keeping them safe and making sure they did the right things. Even though Dre did what he had to do for his family, he knew it was wrong in the eyes of his parents and God. He asked his parents to watch over him, and guide him through his decisions. He wished there was a way they could show him a sign from heaven. He needed to know that they understood that he had no choice but to resort to something that they would never approve of.

"I love you," he said as he wiped a tear from his eyes. It was always hard for him to say goodbye. He promised to come back next week for a special visit. It was his mother's birthday and he would not miss coming with her favorite roses.

Dre lay in his bed staring at the number that Sterling had given him so long ago. He promised himself and his grandmother that he would stay away from him because he was bad news.

As the cab driver approached the area where Sterling lived, Dre thought that he had made a mistake writing down the directions that he had given him. He was in an area of Miami that he never knew existed. The subdivision only had about ten homes in it and each one was huge. Dre had only seen houses like this on the "Lifestyles of the Rich and Famous." He knew Sterling had money but he had no idea that he was rich. The driver waited at the end of the driveway as instructed by Dre while he went to get the money for the fare from Sterling. He could not believe the size of this house. It was two stories with iron

balconies and large white columns. There was a
flowing water fountain with a large marble statue in
the center. Parked in the driveway were a brand
new Cadillac and a black corvette. As he climbed
the stairs to the mansion his heart began to pound.
He was extremely nervous about his visit with
Sterling. The large door opened.

"Hey Dre, I'm glad you're here man, come
on in," said Sterling, as he went out to pay the
driver. Dre stood astounded in the foyer as he
waited for his return. The inside of the house was
even more fabulous than the outside. Several people
sat around a table in the living room snorting
cocaine.

"Come on, I'm in the backyard. Just let me
finish up this call and I'll be right with you," he said
as he led Dre through the house and out by the pool.
"Sit! Killer, stay," he commanded two well-trained
Doberman pinschers. "It's okay man. They won't
attack unless I tell them to." Dre was uneasy at the
sight of the huge dogs that took their places by their
master's side. 2 beautiful women sat in the Jacuzzi.
Sterling offered Dre something cold to drink as he
finished his call. As Dre looked around at all of the
wealth that he appeared to have he couldn't help but
to feel a slight animosity towards Sterling. Even
though his father had always taken very good care
of him and his mother, he still felt abandoned by his

biological father who obviously was living the good life.

Sterling ended his call smiling as he looked at his son. He too was nervous about why Dre wanted to see him all of a sudden, but he was also happy that he finally called.

"It's good to see you man. How's everything?"

"Well, I'm not going to beat around the bush about why I needed to talk to you," he said nervously.

"What's up man? What's going on, talk to me…" Sterling could see that Dre had something serious on his mind, but he did not want to pressure him.

"I need your help."

"Okay, what do you need, money? I'd be glad to give you…," Dre interrupted. Sterling sat back to allow him to talk. "I will take care of my own family, not that you know anything about that," he sarcastically said. "What I need from you is a loan."

"Okay," he slowly said. "How much do you need?" Dre looked Sterling straight in the eyes. "I need…a pound."

Sterling, not sure of what he heard asked Dre to repeat himself. "I need a pound of marijuana and I'll pay you for it after I make the money back." Sterling frowned, "First of all I don't sell weed. That's just not my game. Sterling could not believe what he was asking of him. He also disapproved. He insisted that Dre explain his situation in detail. Sterling told him that he would do anything to help him, but he refused to help him get involved in selling drugs. He wanted more from his son, and he'd hoped that he would be a much better man than he was. Dre, irritated at Sterling's questioning stood up and blurted, "Oh, you want to be a father now huh? Listen, if you don't want to help me, I'll find someone who will!" Dre angrily headed for the door.

"Dre wait! I have told you the circumstances surrounding why I wasn't involved in your life. It wasn't me; it was your mother and grandmother that insisted that I stay away. I believed in my heart that I was doing the right thing. Don't tell me that I never gave a damn! I did then, and I still do now. Because I love you is why I don't want you to end up like me. You have no idea how dangerous of a game this is. People that sell drugs aren't nice people, they will kill you about their money. Myself included." Sterling had hoped to frighten some sense into him but Dre was a strong-willed young man.

Finally after the two men argued their points, and Dre continued to stand his ground with Sterling, he agreed to help him. He sat for hours and told Dre the ends and outs, the do's and the don'ts to selling drugs. He realized that Dre had his mind made up and he was determined to get the drugs and the knowledge from whomever he could. Sterling was afraid that he would end up with someone on the streets that would hurt him. Dre insisted that he always pay him for the drugs that he received. As much as Sterling hated to agree to be his son's drug dealer, he did. He was involved in much heavier distribution, such as cocaine and heroin. He made Dre promise that he would only sell drugs and never use them.

"I guess you would know huh?" snarled Dre.

"I deserved that," replied Sterling, "But I've stopped using for a while now."

It wasn't long before the trio had a perfect system going. Since Domino already had a good rapport with the people on his grandmother's side of town, that's where he set up his area. T.J. concentrated on another area and his school. He was attending a smaller university because

academically he wasn't ready for the larger ones.
T.J. was dyslexic and despite his scholarship offers,
he felt intimidated. Dre stood in the background of
the operation. He continued to work for Mr.
Frederick, but only on the weekends. He did not
like the idea of letting people know that he was
involved with anything illegal. Domino on the
other hand enjoyed the status it brought him. He
loved to brag and show off. Dre had to remind his
friend constantly that they had to remain low-key so
no one would suspect anything. Because Dre
remained a silent partner, and other than his two
best friends, no one else was aware of his
involvement, he knew that if he were to find himself
in trouble that one of them was responsible. It
wasn't that he was worried about them snitching,
just that Dre's identity was sworn secrecy among
them. They each bore a tattoo on their arm of a
cobra symbolizing their organization.

Dre insisted on keeping things very simple.
He wasn't trying to get rich; he was mainly
concerned with a descent income for himself and
his family. At first, he was only averaging around
an extra $500 per week. This was fine for him. He
felt that less was better. He wanted to keep
clientele at a minimum. The fewer people knowing
about them, kept their business out of the streets.
However, because of Domino's greed and power

hungry appetite, profits grew quickly. After only three months in business, Dre was netting close to $1000 weekly. This scared him. The money was wonderful, but the risks were too much. He insisted that Domino slow down.

With the money that Dre was now making he insisted on moving the family in a much safer neighborhood. He found a nice three-bedroom apartment that wasn't too expensive and closer to his Uncle Terry, who along with his wife helped with his grandmother. Of course his grandmother and Uncle Terry were a little suspicious of the money but Dre always managed to make her feel comfortable. He kept some of his money in a savings account. He knew he only wanted to do this until he graduated next year, because of his grades he was able to get a partial academic scholarship but still needed more money for college. Dre refused to spend his money on flashy clothes and jewelry like Domino did. He and T.J. managed to keep a level head about what they were doing and future plans. T.J. realized his chances of being selected for the pros were slim, so he planned to open a restaurant in a few years with his money. Domino spent every dime he had trying to impress women and the local hoodlums.

After about a year Dre wasn't getting his supply from Sterling anymore. Sterling's fast life of women and partying was catching up with him and he began using cocaine again. Sterling assured his son that he could handle the drugs but Dre was beginning to notice that Sterling's life as well as his business was spiraling down.

(Four Years Later…) Dre unbuttoned his suit jacket as the choir finished their B-selection. Fans were moving briskly in the air as sweaty church members tried to remain cool. Miami's summers always put a strain on the small church's small air conditioning unit.

"A new unit," Dre thought to himself. That would be his monthly tithing donation to the church on behalf of his family. Dre has always been very generous to the church. He was thankful for his many blessings and that God had brought him so far without any danger coming to him. Even though he felt like a real hypocrite sitting in church, clapping his hands and praising God, he knew he was true and sincere, and that God knew his heart. Very seldom Dre missed a Sunday in church. His grandmother although very frail now insisted that he and his sisters were there.

His heart was heavy. Last night he phoned Sterling to invite him to church with him but he refused as usual. Dre believed that if he could just get him into the house of the Lord, that God would take care of the rest. Sterling started using again and Dre knew he needed real help, and fast. Sterling was sinking further into his addiction with cocaine. For days he would lock himself in his bedroom and shoot poison into his failing veins. Somehow, he had managed to shoot and snort all of his money. Sterling was no longer the strong lion many had looked up to and even feared for so many years. All the fine jewelry, homes, and clothes...gone. The women, the parties, the friends...are now all gone. He now lives in a one room furnished hotel apartment where he stays day in and day out. His only source of income came from the little money Dre would give him back from the pounds of marijuana that he was selling. Sterling didn't mess with weed, it was the hard stuff, the cocaine, that he needed, and for so long he was using the very same supply that he was trying to sell which created issues with his supplier.

GRADUATION DAY

A large crowd of well-wishers and graduates gathered outside of the auditorium,

"Say cheese," gushed Uncle Terry as he took a photo of Dre standing proudly with his diploma in his cap & gown.

"Okay, get one with your sisters now," said Uncle Terry. DeeDee and Shannon raced to his side. "Yeah, that's going to be a good one," he said.

"I'm so proud of my big brother," DeeDee said as she hugged him.

"You're next sis!"

"I know, one more year, I can't wait!"

"Good job man, our family's first college graduate, your mother is smiling from ear to ear in heaven right now," said Uncle Terry as he also embraced his nephew. "Boy I wish she could be here for this."

"Yeah, I know. She'd be crying like a baby," replied Dre.

"There go my boy," yells TJ as he breaks through the crowd approaching the group. DeeDee blushes. He gives Dre some dap. "Boy you looked nervous up there."

"I was man. Nervous and excited at the same time," said Dre. "I thought this day would never come."

"Next Law School," said TJ.

"You know it!" smiled Dre.

"With our hood alone you'll stay busy," laughed TJ.

"...and you'll get rich off your boy Domino alone," laughed Uncle Terry.

Dre and TJ snickered. "Where is that fool anyway?" asked Dre.

"Who knows man, ain't no telling with him, he said he was coming," replied TJ.

"We'll just start the celebration without him, he'll catch up to us later I'm sure. Hey Unc, you comin' to the restaurant for some drinks?" asked TJ.

"I wish I could TJ but me and my wife need to go check on mama for a while. You know she hasn't been doing too good and I don't like her at the house too long by herself." "Ya'll have a good time."

But we will be checking out your new spot real soon, "I heard it was nice man," replied Uncle Terry. Congratulations!

"Thanks Unc, we've been blessed to be so busy since the grand opening last month. It's a dream come true for me."

"Well I'm proud of both of you two young men. You kept your noses clean, stayed out of trouble and made something of yourselves. You could have been a statistic and slung dope like the rest of these knuckleheads but you didn't. I'm damn proud," said Uncle Terry. Dre and TJ glanced at one another.

"…Well look, ya'll have fun tonight and don't drink too much." Uncle Terry continued.

"I wanna go with ya'll," yelled Shannon. Dre chuckled. "You are going with us little girl," laughed Uncle Terry. "Not tonight little sis, this is strictly for the grown and sexy," said DeeDee.

"You barely made the cut yourself Dee," laughed Uncle Terry. "Who...I'm 21 now Unc, I'm good," smiled DeeDee. TJ grinned, as he looked her up and down.

"Like I said, you barely made the cut," repeated Uncle Terry. He gives TJ and Dre some dap, "Ya'll be safe."

"We will," said Dre. "Tell grandma I love her and we won't be home too late.

"You know she'll be waiting up for ya'll," said Carol, Terry's wife. "Like always," said Dee.

TJ glances at DeeDee in his rearview mirror as she smiles at him from the back seat. He glances back in the rearview mirror, "we have all night." DeeDee blushes, Dre frowns as he catches TJ looking at DeeDee. "Eyes on the road nigga, eyes on the road," said Dre. TJ looks shocked, "What? Man I got this," he argued. "Yeah, whatever," smirked Dre as he looks at DeeDee in the back seat. "I'm not stupid DeeDee," he yelled! "What are you talking about Dre?" she whined. He again looks at TJ with a serious face. "Not that one TJ, that's my little sister and for the last time she's off limits to you."

"Dre, you're tripping! First of all I'm not a little girl anymore, second, you're not my father, and you don't control me," snapped DeeDee. He cuts his eyes at both of them, "I control more than you think I do."

The sound of glass breaking startles Eva as she's awakened from a nap in her favorite chair. She lowers the volume on her television. "Dre, is that you?" Her eyes widened in fear, "How did you get in here?" The sound of gunfire can be heard from the outside of the house.

"I'm hungry daddy," whined Terry's little girl from the backseat of the car. "I know boo, I'm sure Nana has a feast waiting for us," said Terry as he pulls into the driveway. His wife Carol frowns as she sees the front door halfway opened. "That's odd; Ms. Eva would never leave her door opened like that..." Terry rushes toward the house.

"I did it. I got my bachelors and I'm on my way to becoming the man ya'll raised me to be," says Dre as he stands in front of his parents headstones. He's still wearing his commencement gown, now open, he continues "I know it was always your dream for me to go to law school at Berkeley, but I'm going to stay here at home so that I can take care of everyone. University of Miami has a great law program so no big deal." His eyes fill with tears. "God I hope you're proud of me. I want to keep believing that you are still with us watching over us like an angel. Keeping us safe..."

DeeDee leans over the front seat, whispering in TJ's ear. "So are you still scared of my brother?"

He smirks, "I'm not scared of your brother, I just respect him that's all." She smirks, seductively leaning back, "Um huh."

Dre enters the car. "You okay bruh?" he asks. "Yeah, I'm good man. We got time for one more stop?" "Yeah, no problem, the party doesn't start without you anyway," chuckles TJ.

"I want to go and give Nana my diploma. It's just as much hers as it is mine. Plus I know she probably made all my favorites." TJ pulls off, once again, looking in the mirror.

Eva's house has been ransacked and Carol is consoling her children in the kitchen. Terry is tearfully holding his mother in his arms as Dre enters. "Nana" Dre whispered. As he sees her blood soaked dress, Terry, on the floor, continues to cradle her in his arms gently rocking her. "Why did they do this to you mama?" he sobs.

THE END OF AN ERA

Despite everything Dre continued to work hard in law school. DeeDee was preparing to graduate from the University of Miami this June and was now on her way to becoming an FBI agent. Shannon was about to enter into her first year at Florida A&M University, with hopes of getting into medical school.

He knew his grandmother's death was his fault and robbery was the motive. Each week since the robbery he would call the detective but still no leads. Uncle Terry hadn't been to the house since that day and his wife was worried about his mental state. Terry couldn't put his finger on it but he had a feeling that Dre knew more than he let on.

Even though he felt extremely guilty Dre had accomplished everything he set out to do. Provided for his family and kept them together for ten years. He continued to use the money he made in a positive way. No fancy cars or clothes, choosing instead to put himself and his two sisters through college. Over the next year and a half Dre was even more determined to stop selling drugs.

Soon he would be a big criminal attorney, his parent's dream. Of course his dream was to also be a professional basketball player, but unfortunately his injuries ended those hopes years ago. He had no more use for his dark side. The pieces of the puzzle were finally coming together and it was time to quit the game for good.

T.J. shared his feelings. He too had profited from this life of crime but was now pretty successful in the restaurant business. He loved Dre like a brother. "When you're done, I'm done," he always told Dre. Domino on the other hand loved the power and money that selling drugs brought him.

"I'm the game, and the game is me," he often told them. He felt right at home in the streets, and was intrigued by the danger. After all these years he was still the same Domino. Always in some shit or ready to kill someone because he thought they didn't show him enough respect. They were so ready to end their involvement with him. Although they still loved him like a brother, they hated his evil ways. Just recently Domino had almost gotten the three of them killed at a local nightclub. He apparently got into an altercation with four guys over some girl earlier that night. As the three were about to leave the club a car pulled up from out of nowhere and opened fire. T.J. was hit in the stomach. After 9 hours of surgery and four days of touch and go, the doctors felt pretty sure that he was going to pull through. Domino felt terrible about what happened to his best friend and vowed to get even. Dre tried to discourage him from starting a street war but he was determined that they would pay, and sure enough, about three weeks later the four men responsible for the drive by turned up dead in an apartment in Ft. Lauderdale. Police marked it as a gang related incident, but the dominoes found in each the mouths of the victims was enough for Dre and T.J. to confirm who did it. This was Dre's last straw. Drugs were ruining everything and everyone around him.

After leaving church one Sunday, Dre headed to Sterling's apartment to tell him he was done. He didn't bother to call because he knew he would probably be there either sleeping or getting high.

As Dre entered the lobby of Sterling's apartment building, he could smell the stench of urine and trash in the halls. The sounds of babies crying and loud music echoed in his ears.

"From sugar to shit," he murmured as he shook his head in disgust. He couldn't believe Sterling had actually sunk so low. As he approached Sterling's door his heart raced because he had just about become Sterling's only source of money because no one else would deal with him because of his habit. He knew that Sterling would be upset with him but he was just going to have to understand. He remembered back when he first went to Sterling for his help, and he always told him that anytime he could quit. Things are different now and Sterling was depending on him.

"Open up Sterling, it's Dre," he said as he knocked on the door. He listened for a second then he reached for the door knob. The door was unlocked so Dre opened it and went inside. "Hey man, you ain't in Coconut Grove anymore, you better start locking these doors." He heard water running in the bathroom so he walked over to the door and knocked. "Hey pops what's up? You stinking it up in there again?" Once again, no response. "Hey man when you get out of the tub we need to take a ride or something, you know, get out of this room for a minute." He went over to the refrigerator to get something cold to drink.

Dre was becoming curious as to why he hadn't heard anything from Sterling and he had been running bath water for a while now. He wondered if Sterling had possibly passed out in the bathroom. He turned the knob but the door was locked. "Sterling, are you all right in there man?" Suddenly Dre looked down at his feet, and noticed water coming from underneath the door. He panicked. He realized Sterling was in trouble so he tried to kick the door open. "Pops! …Say something man," he said as he kicked the door a few more times. Finally the door flew open. "Oh shit…no man….no what'd you do man," he screamed. Sterling was floating face down in the overflowing tub with his hands and feet tied behind his back. His throat had been slashed and there was blood everywhere. Someone had murdered Sterling, but who, and for what? It was apparent that he was a junkie and had no money. Dre was seriously upset. The sight of Sterling laying in that tub of blood made him throw up all over the floor.

"What was your relationship to the deceased," asked one of the police officers. Dre was still noticeably upset as he stared into the bathroom. "He was…my father," he paused, Sterling Lanier. He had never addressed Sterling as his father to anyone before. He may have called him Pops from time to time, but he always regarded James Snipes as his father. As he watched the coroner zip the body bag and toss Sterling onto the stretcher he wondered if this had all been a bad dream. Dre glanced at the dresser next to him and noticed a small black and white photo. It was kind of worn, and it had a corner missing. It was a picture of Sterling and Dre's mother, holding him when he was a little baby. Apparently he had been keeping this old photo of them during happier times. "He still loved her," he said aloud. "All these years and she was still on his mind." This made Dre feel real good inside, to know that his father really did love his mother. "You may not have always been there for me pop, but you came right when I needed you…Thank you, I love you man," he said as he placed his hand on the body bag. The coroner motioned to Dre as if to say he was out of time and began rolling Sterling's body out of the door. Dre felt so empty inside. He wiped the tears that were falling down his cheek, put the picture of him and his parent in his pocket, and walked out of the door.

The sun had not yet gone completely down and the children were already out trick-or-treating. In fact, there was a batman, a clown, and a skeleton on the porch waiting when DeeDee arrived home from work.

"Trick or treat," screamed the trio in unison, as she climbed the stairs to the porch. "Oh boy, look at you guys. Wait a second let me open the door, I think I've got something in here for you." DeeDee unlocked the door, grabbed the mail from the mailbox and went inside. She grabbed the bowl of candy from the coffee table and gave each kid two pieces.

"Say "Thank you," scolded the children's mother, as they walked back down the driveway.

"Thank you," screamed the children.

"You're welcome cutie pies. Don't eat too much candy," smiled DeeDee. She loved kids and hoped to one day have a house full of her own. She was more than ready to get married, and start a family, but her long time boyfriend of three years, also Dre's best friend, T.J. was still a secret. Dre always forbade DeeDee to get involved with T.J. Although he loved and trusted him like a brother, he didn't think he was right for his little sister. Many times over the years Dre threatened his friend about his sister. Whenever he became suspicious he would confront T.J. and T.J. was never actually afraid of Dre, but he respected him and was smart enough to know that he would probably kill him about his sister. But DeeDee on the other hand was becoming fed up with her brother's over protectiveness. She was in love with T.J. and was tired of sneaking around. Many times she would threaten him that if he wouldn't tell Dre about their relationship then she would, but he always managed to convince her that he would do it when the time was right. He was sure that Dre would feel differently about him and his sister now that he wasn't dealing drugs anymore or putting DeeDee in danger.

As DeeDee passed out more candy to the children the phone began to ring. It was her sweetheart.

"Hey sexy," T.J. said.

"Hey baby, I was just thinking about you."

"Oh yeah, what were you thinking about, my sexy body and how you can't wait until tonight?"

"No silly. I was thinking about more than just tonight. I was imagining us being married and having babies."

"DeeDee, don't get started again okay, we have to be patient."

"I've been patient for too long. I'm twenty-two years old now, and capable of making my own decisions. I love my brother and he's always been there for me but it's time I stood up to him."

"Okay stand up to him, you gone get us both knocked the fuck out," joked T.J.

"I'm serious T.J. I'm telling Dre about us once and for all," she said.

"Look, we'll talk about it tonight okay? My cell phone bill is already sky high. What time will you be at my house anyway?"

"Why?"

"Girl stop playing, what time now?"

"Don't you worry about what time I'm going to be there. You just have your ass home and butt naked when I get there," laughed DeeDee.

"I don't know what I'm going to do with you. All right baby, I'll see you later. Love you."

"I love you too," said DeeDee as she hung up the phone.

"Who was that Dee," asked Dre, startling her.

"Boy, you scared me, I didn't hear you come in," she said, trying to change the subject.

"Yeah, I just walked in, but who were you telling that you loved them" he asked. Trying to think quickly she blurted out...

"Damn Dre, it was Ricky, and why are you all in my conversation anyway?" she said with a little attitude. Ricky was a guy she went out with in college a few times.

"Ricky, I thought you hated him. When did ya'll get back together?"

"We're really not together, you know I'm just juicing his ass," laughed DeeDee. She knew she'd better change the subject fast before he asked anymore questions.

"Dre, there's something for you on your bed. His bar exam scores were back. She did all she could to keep from opening his mail herself. He'd been checking the mailbox every day and today it finally came.

Dre slowly walked out his room holding the opened letter down at his side. DeeDee met her brother in the hallway full of anticipation, watching for any expression from him. Dre said nothing and showed no emotion. Instead, he clinched the letter tightly in his fist and stared at the floor.

"What's wrong Dre," she asked with a tremble in her voice. She knew how hard he'd worked and studied for years to become a lawyer. The long hours in the library, reading and researching, up all night long cramming, only to be up again for an eight o'clock class. She saw that his eyes were filling with water which triggered her own set of tears. Dre fell to his knees. After quickly skimming the contents out loud, DeeDee stopped abruptly.

"Oh my God," she screamed, as she dropped down to embrace her sobbing brother. "Thank you Jesus. Thank you Lord! You did it Dre. Yes, yes, yes, you really did it!" The two sat in the middle of the floor holding each other and crying tears of joy. "My big brother the lawyer!"

Morning didn't come soon enough for Dre. He could hardly wait to visit his parent's graves and share the good news. Today was the first day of the rest of his life. He was excited about starting with Nelson, Whitaker, and Whitaker, a large firm in South Beach. They were equally excited about welcoming him aboard. They knew he was a hard worker and very intelligent. He graduated in the top five percent of his class and the firm had been interested in him ever since.

"I did it ma," cried Dre, as he knelt down and placed two dozen yellow roses on her grave. Dre believed in his heart that she smiled every time he brought her yellow roses. "Your oldest son is now a lawyer. Your dream; yours, and pops... I hope you are proud of me," he said as he began to weep. "My life is about to change forever, I promise you momma. I will do my best to live the way you and pops raised me to. Now that we are all grown up and doing fine, my job is now complete."

Dre was sincere in his promise to his parents. It had nearly been a month since Sterling was killed and Dre never looked back on selling drugs since. Even though Domino continued to try to persuade him to continue, Dre refused. For the first time in a long while he felt free, and he loved it.

THE VISITOR

Life was wonderful. Nearly one year had passed and Dre was successfully settling into his new firm. His office sat on the 23rd floor of a high rise building in lovely South Beach. He enjoyed sitting at his desk starring through his enormous glass window. Pictures of his parents, sisters, and grandmother sat neatly across the room on top of his credenza. He proudly displayed his diploma in a beautiful gold frame on the wall above it. Oriental throw rugs matched his emerald green leather couch which served as his bed on many nights. Dre was enjoying his criminal practice although he was only given smaller cases. He didn't mind because he knew he had to pay his dues.

"Mr. Lanier...excuse me, Mr. Lanier." Dre was startled by his secretary's voice as he was gazing out the window.

"I'm sorry Lanora, what is it?"

"There is a Mr. Sanchez here to see you. He does not have an appointment."

"Mr. Sanchez," he said with a puzzled look.

"Auhh, that's fine Lanora, I have some time before my next arraignment, send him in," he interrupted. Another consultation he thought as the door slowly opened. In walked Angel, the son of Carlos Sanchez. Dre had no seen him in over six years. Sterling and Carlos had taken them on a boat trip in the Caribbean where they became good friends.

"What in the hell...man what are you doing here," said Dre as he stood up to greet the tall, dark and very handsome Columbian.

"Business my friend, you could say family business." Angel had taken control of the cartel since his father had been kidnapped and assassinated about a year before Sterling was killed.

"Hey man, I'm sorry about your pops," said Dre. Sterling loved him like a brother and he often said he was the only man he could trust. You know he was killed too," said Dre. "Yeah, I know about that, that's too bad," said Angel. Angel was as handsome as his father, only taller, about 6'4" or 6'5". "Actually, your father is why I'm here today." Dre sat back in his chair with a puzzled look.

"I'm listening." Angel walked over to the window and gazed at the ocean. "Dre, I'm sure you are aware that Sterling was a major dealer her in south Florida for my family for many years. At least up until, well, you know he had a problem. My father tolerated his behavior and his stealing from him for a long time. I guess he hoped that one day he would change." Angel paused as if he were thinking about his dead father. "Well, anyway, since my father's death, I've taken over and I changed a few things. I know you sold drugs for years for Sterling," said Angel.

"Well, not really," said Dre in a nervous whisper. He was surprised that Angel knew about that.

"Look Dre, I already know all about you, T.J., and your "out of control" friend...uuh...Domino." Dre was beginning to get very uncomfortable with this conversation. That part of his life was behind him and he wanted to forget about it.

"Listen man, I'm not really sure what you're getting at or why you're here but I'm very busy and further more I'm out of that business. As you can see, I am an attorney now and very content with my new life. Angel laughed as he sat on the edge of Dre's desk.

"Last year I made over 200 million dollars...yeah, 19913 was a good year for me, but I intend to double that this year. I need you my friend to control the entire southeastern region, Florida, Georgia, and Alabama for now. You could keep your little lawyer job for show if you want to, but think of the cash you will make with me," smiled Angel.

"I've already told you, I'm not interested. I sold drugs to provide for my family and pay for my college. I have successfully put myself and my sisters through school so my job is done." Angel leaned towards him and starred him straight in the eyes. Dre could see chrome plated 9mm in his pants as his coat moved.

"I'm not asking you, I'm telling you, so the way I see it, you don't have much choice. You're a drug dealer whether you want to admit it or not. You belong to the cartel; you owe the cartel for allowing you to do what you did for all those years. You can thank Sterling because you've inherited the family business." Dre stood up and pushed Angel out of his face.

"Get the fuck out of my office. Dre said calmly. You don't threaten me, I didn't inherit shit, nor do I belong to you or the damn cartel," he said as he stood up and faced Angel. Angel snickered at Dre as if to insult his manhood.

"I see you are just as stupid as your father, and you see what defiance got him. He had a job to do. He was told to sell our cocaine not use it. He stole from my father…he stole from me…millions of dollars. That nigger had to die. I'm not my father, I hated his black ass and he apparently forgot who was in charge." Dre fell back into his chair and starred at Angel in disbelief. He could not believe what was being said to him. Angel murdered Sterling in cold blood.

"Oh by the way how are those two lovely sister of yours," said Angel with a demonic look in his eyes. "I hear Shannon wants to become a doctor and she's going to a university in Tallahassee." Dre was astonished. He knows everything about me and my family he thought to himself. How did he even know I had sisters?

"You know how dangerous campuses have gotten. Wouldn't it be a shame if something were to happen to her up there?"

"If you dare touch one hair," screamed Dre as he stood in anger.

"You're going to do what you punk? I know you're not trying to threaten me because I'll kill you, and your ugly ass sisters before lunch. Don't fuck with me nigger! I can erase your ass just like

Sterling," he said as he turned up his mouth and gritted his teeth.

Silence filled the room. Angel reached down and picked up a piece of candy from a crystal dish on Dre's desk.

"Ooohh chocolate, my favorite…you mind?" Dre just stared out his window and cracked his knuckles, something he often did when he was nervous and upset. "Saturday, I want you in Columbia, there's a lot you have to learn. There is a major difference between marijuana and cocaine. Here's your ticket," he said as he threw an envelope on the desk. "There will be someone waiting to pick you up, and expect to be there a least a week."

"You've got it all figured out don't you Angel? How in the hell do you expect me to be able to pick up and leave my firm for a week? I'm not a drug dealer, I'm a lawyer!" Angel smiled at Dre,

"No my friend …no matter how hard you try…you'll always be a drug dealer, only pretending to be a lawyer. Angel stood up, grabbed a few more pieces of chocolate, and headed for the door. "If you miss that flight, you'd better start swimming to Columbia. If my driver comes back without you, I promise you an early retirement," he said as he opened the door. Lanora was sitting at her desk typing on her computer. Angel winked at her, causing her to blush with embarrassment. Angel, although a shrewd and sinister monster, was a handsome and charming lady's man. Lanora immediately began checking her hair and makeup when she noticed him preparing to leave her bosses office.

"Hey man it was good seeing you again, and I hope to see you real soon," he said as he starred deep into Dre's eyes. Dre felt a burning sensation in the pit of his stomach as he watched Angel walk out of his office and exit onto the elevator. Out of frustration, Dre picked up the candy dish and threw it at the door. He believed Angel when he said he would kills him and his family, but what was he to do. He could not run, Angel apparently knew everything about him. The cartel was powerful and deadly so he knew he had to go along with Angel's demands, at least until he figured out how to get out of this.

"Why me," he said to himself as he sand into his chair. He knew nothing about that aspect of the drug business nor was he interested in learning, so how was Angel expecting him to control any entire region of the country. "This thing is way too big," he thought to himself. Could Angel be right about him never being any more than a drug dealer?

Dre was devastated at the thought. All this time he thought he was only doing what he had to do to survive. He never intended for this life to consume him. He felt like a caged animal waiting to be shot. He began ripping up papers that he had sitting on his desk. He had so much rage inside of him, "He killed Sterling," he whispered, "That mother-fucker killed my father!"

Dre sat and stared at the airline ticket Angel left on his desk for almost thirty minutes. Thoughts of he and Sterling's last days filled his head. Once Angel took over the cartel, he set out to clean up the organization and get rid of those who were weak. Sterling had been stealing from Angel's father for years but Carlos let him get away with it because of his loyalty to him. Sterling saved Carlos' life over fifteen years ago during an earlier assassination attempt. His car had been rigged with a bomb and Sterling detected it after his bodyguards had overlooked it. After that Sterling was treated like one of his sons and Angel always despised him for that.

"Lanora," Dre called to his secretary, "Cancel all of my appointments, I'm taking the rest of the day off. I'm not feeling well."

The next six months were devoted to setting up this $75 million dollar operation. Dre sent T.J. to Alabama to run that area and Domino to Atlanta to set up business there. Taking over those areas wasn't going to be easy because it was already being controlled by other groups. The Miami boys were also strong in south Florida, but the cartel quickly and brutally got rid of all the bosses in those organizations.

Through all of this Dre managed to juggle his law career. He refused to believe that he was just as bad as Angel was. He worked hard to get where he was and nothing was about to stop him. He was determined to beat Angel at his own game. T.J. wasn't at all excited about moving to Alabama and getting back to the streets. He was especially upset about leaving DeeDee. He was preparing to open his second restaurant on Miami's south beach. Domino on the other hand couldn't have been more pleased. This meant big money and more power for him. Angel wasn't at all particular about Domino working for him. He felt he was too militant and gung ho, and could bring attention to the cartel. Angel was definitely right. Domino was heavily involved in illegal gambling, prostitution, and was know on the streets to be a hit man. There had already been an incident where Domino and T.J. had been out partying at a club in Atlanta. Domino had gotten into a fight with another know dealer from Memphis. Because the owner knew Domino and he was a big spender in his club, he threw the other guy and his crew out. Later on that morning when the club was closing, Domino and T.J. were in the parking lot walking towards their car when three shots rang out. When the smoke cleared Domino was on the ground. He had been shot once in the leg. The gunman was identified as Mark Grant, the same individual that had been thrown out of the nightclub. Domino spent two days in the hospital recovering from his wounds.

Dre assured Angel that he would keep him under control. He knew Domino was a bit crazy and caused trouble everywhere he went, but he also realized he didn't need a "soft nigga" on the streets of Atlanta. Plus he knew he could trust him. Angel swore the first time Domino got out of hand that Dre would be accountable.

DeeDee was able to keep Dre informed about inside operations at the bureau. She worried so much about her brother and his involvement with this Colombian. For years the DEA had been unsuccessful in obtaining something concrete on Angel. His cartel was too strong and had managed to infiltrate the bureau. Together they realized that they were going to have to come up with a plan to destroy Angel before he destroyed them.

Angel was definitely right. Over the next year he grossed millions from the operation. Each month Angel sent Dre 1000 keys of cocaine which he dispersed equally between himself, Domino, and T.J. The cocaine was brought into Miami by way of cargo ships and airplanes. Dre still insisted no one else was to know his identity so twice a month Domino and T.J would fly to Miami, to arrange for their drivers to pick up their shipments, while dropping off hundreds of thousands to Dre. Dre knew that if anything ever happened that only those two could finger him.

It took them days to separate $100's, $50's, $20's, $10's, and so on. Then it took them another 10 to 12 hours to run the cash through the money counter and bag it up in $50,000 increments. Dre never thought he could hate money as he was beginning to. Many nights he would fall asleep on piles of it too exhausted to go on. He never got enough sleep. Many nights after counting money, he had to spend hours researching for cases. Sometimes if he was lucky he could get about two hours on his couch in the office before he had to appear in court. For this reason he always kept extra suits and shirts in his closet at work.

Each month when Dre met with Angel, he was sure it was his last. Although he himself had made a couple of million dollars he was more than ready to end his relationship with the Columbian. Unfortunately with every deal came more promises and excuses.

"Six more months and I will consider letting you go. I can't just stop making money just because you don't want to. I need to find someone to replace you…someone I can trust to make millions for me." Dre was finally realizing he had inherited this nightmare from Sterling and he was trapped.

LOVE AT FIRST SIGHT

It wasn't often that Dre was able to have lunch away from the firm. He arranged his schedule so he could take Tim, his fraternity brother that graduated law school with him to lunch for his birthday. The two had been growing pretty close over the years. Tim was a single and very attractive bachelor. He and Dre often worked out and played ball together on the weekends or whenever the two of them weren't busy with a case. Ever since T.J. and Domino moved away, Dre longed for a close buddy and Tim was thee.

Dre parked his black convertible Porsche 911 next to Tim's white Mercedes 500SL. Tim was a civil attorney with Gayle and Associates in Ft. Lauderdale, just twenty minutes from Dre's office in Miami.

"Hello Mr. Lanier," smiled Cindy, Tim's long-legged receptionist. She's had an obvious crush on Dre for some time now, and made him a little uncomfortable every time he came to the office. The two actually went out for dinner once before but they didn't hit it off and he never called her again. In fact, he was forced to change his cell phone number because she constantly called and left messages on his voicemail.

"Hey Cindy, is Tim ready? We have 2:30 reservations at the Pier."

"I'm coming," hollered Tim from his office.

"Just have a seat, he's finishing up with a client," said Cindy.

After about fifteen minutes Dre was beginning to become impatient. Cindy was just about to talk his ear off and she kept bending over to get her files so Dre could get a good look at her legs. Every thirty seconds he would look down at his watch and glance down the hall towards Tim's office door. The office was a bit warm so he took his suit coat off and laid it on the chair next to him. He looked absolutely stunning in his blue Armani double-breasted suit and he sensed Cindy staring.

Suddenly the office door opened and an angel appeared in front of him. Tim had his arm around the troubled beauty consoling her. She appeared to have been crying. Dre couldn't help but to stare at her. Her hair was jet black and wavy, and her skin was golden bronze. He has always had a weakness for Latin women, but this goddess was especially overwhelming to him.

"Call me in the morning Bianca and I should have some more information for you. Cheer up honey, everything is going to work out I promise," said Tim. Bianca glanced over at Dre as she headed for the door. He couldn't take his eyes off her even when she noticed him staring. She nodded as she said hello. Her scent was a sweet stinging to his nose. He quickly rose to his feet to open the door for her.

"Hello, I'm Andre Lanier," he said in a shy and nervous voice, as he reached out for her hand.

"Nice to meet you, Mr. Lanier, I'm Bianca Dupree, and I'm sorry but I must run."

"Oh, the pleasure was all mine. I hope you have a nice day okay," he said as he watched her walk across the parking lot and get into her minivan.

"She's a piece isn't she man," said Tim as he grabbed his suit jacket from the stand. Dre was still watching her walk across the parking lot and get into her minivan.

"I have to know her. Is she your client, what's the deal?" said Dre anxiously. Tim looked at Dre with surprise. He had never seen Dre act this way over a beautiful woman before usually it was the other way around women were always pursuing Dre. He had a few relationships here and there, but nothing serious. He never really had the time for a real girlfriend, and whenever they started to demand to know where he was going or who he was with he cut them loose. He didn't like them getting too personal or hanging around too much.

Bianca Dupree was a foster mother for abandoned and abused crack babies. She had temporary custody of six children ranging from ages of ten on down to six months old. Tim was trying to help her gain permanent legal custody of them and because she was single and had low income, she was denied. She worked part-time as a hair stylist in Boca Raton.

"Yeah she's one sweet and kind-hearted girl, and if I wasn't such a dog I'd probably try and hit it myself," chuckled Tim.

"Is she married," asked Dre.

"Nope."

Dre rubbed his chin and smiled at his friend.

"Hey man, I've never asked you for anything before,"

"No, before you even ask," interrupted Tim. "You know how I feel about match making. I wound up in the middle of you and Cindy's mess."

"I'm not asking you to hook me up, just put in a good word for me, and look out for a brother man. Just let me know when she's coming back or something, and I'll be here. That's all you have to do and I'll handle it from there." Tim looked at his desperate friend and laughed.

"Hook me up with your fine ass sister first."

"DeeDee," asked Dre.

"Yeah, DeeDee. You know Shannon's fine as hell too, but she's too young for me." Dre hesitated. He was very protective of his sisters, and he knew Tom was a "love em', and leave em' kind of guy. He thought to himself, "What the hell, DeeDee thinks he's a nerd anyway, she'll never go out with him."

"Okay, deal, I'll hook you up with my sister, but I'm not responsible if she doesn't go for it," Dre said sneakily.

"Hey man, just set the stage and "Big Daddy Tim" will do the rest." The two friends jumped into Dre's car, put the top down, and headed down the beach.

For the next two days Dre did nothing but think of the angel he met in his friend's office. He and Tim had planned for him to bump into her again in his office. Tim called her and arranged for her to come in to sign some paperwork. Dre would just happen to be there.

It was 3:30, Tim expected Bianca to walk in at any minute. Dre waited in Tim's office until she arrived.

"Beep" "Mr. Roberts, Miss Dupree is waiting to see you," said Cindy. "He'll be right out, please have a seat."

"Thank you," she said, as she sat in a large leather chair. She was wearing a red suit with a red and white scarf tied around her neck. Her hair was pinned up with tiny curls hanging in her face. Dre stepped out of Tim's office and sat down across from her. He was dressed a little more casual today, wearing a beige suit with a beige silk tee shirt. He was very nervous. He reached down for a magazine on the table in front of him. Bianca reached at the same time.

"Oh, I'm sorry, go right ahead," Bianca insisted.

"Please, you go ahead, I'd rather sit here and admire you anyway," he said. "Damn man," he thought to himself, "That was corny as hell." Bianca sat up and just looked at him saying nothing. He sensed that he had said the wrong thing.

"Listen Bianca, may I call you Bianca? I am going to be honest with you. I could sit here and tell you how beautiful you are but I'm not, I know you hear that every day. I came here today just to get to talk to you. Ever since I saw you the other day, I've thought of nothing but you, and I don't even know you. Now I feel like I have made a fool of myself so I will apologize and leave before I stick my foot in my mouth again. It was a pleasure finally talking to you, and I'm sorry again for being rude." Dre stood up, shook her hand, and walked out of the office. He had never felt so stupid in his life. If she had only spoke, said shut up, or something, he thought. He hopped into his car and drove off. All the way back to his office, he thought of how he had made a fool of himself in front of her. He blew his only chance to go out with her and he'll probably never see her again.

"Ring, ring..." His car phone began to ring.

"Yeah," said Dre.

"Yes, Andre, I would love to go out with you," said the sweetest voice he had ever heard.

"Excuse me," said Dre in confusion. "Who am I speaking with?"

"This is Bianca Dupree. I hope you don't mind me calling your number, Tim gave it to me."

"Thank you," Dre silently said as he looked up towards the sky. "Oh no, I don't mind at all, Miss Dupree, thanks for calling. How did you know that I wanted to take you out?"

"I didn't," she said, "I was only hoping."

Dre smiled because she obviously liked him too.

"Is 7 o'clock okay?"

"7 o'clock is fine" she said. I'll call you later to give you directions to my apartment."

"Great, I'll keep my phone on all day until I hear from you."

"Good-bye sweetie," she said sweetly. That just about caused him to wreck his Porsche. Dre could hardly believe it. The woman of his dreams actually wants to go to dinner with him even after he'd made a fool of himself.

The next three weeks Dre and Bianca grew closer. They spent hours just talking and walking along the beach. Dre really liked this girl. She was different from many of the women he'd been involved with. He felt he could relate to her and that she was on the same accord with him. Not only was she extremely beautiful, but she was smart, caring and funny. Dre loved her sense of humor.

He could sit up all night laughing and gazing into her big brown eyes. She had a heart the size of Texas, and in many ways she reminded Dre of his mother. The way she sacrificed for those children touched him in a big way. She didn't have anything to give them but a lot of love. Something they didn't know until she came into their little lives.

She and the six children lived in a tiny three-bedroom apartment, on a pretty rough side of town. She only worked three days a week so she could spend a lot of time with the children. The twins, Diane and David were the youngest of the bunch. The six-month-old babies were born premature and left in an alley to die. Their twenty-year-old crack addicted mother had three other children already that had been taken by the state. Her wealthy parents that did not like her lifestyle or choice of men also disowned her. She traded her body for drugs so she didn't know the fathers of any of her children. As far as they can tell, their father must have been either Hispanic, or black.

Lindsey was four. She was taken from her mother and father and placed in foster care when she was only two, and Bianca has had her ever since. Not only was she born addicted to crack, but she was physically and sexually abused by her father. Lindsey was Bianca's special baby. Because of her addiction and abuse she was a withdrawn child. She doesn't speak to anyone but Bianca, and even that is not very often. Bianca tries to spend as much time with her to get hr to open up and accept all the love that she has to give her.

Michael is five and physically handicapped. He has only been with Bianca for about four months. His mother used cocaine throughout her pregnancy causing him to be born without any legs. Fortunately he is a high-spirited child with a golden personality. His constant smile is the only thing that keeps Bianca from crying each time she sees him.

Todd is Michael's eight-year-old brother. He is very protective of his little brother and demands to do everything for him. Their mother also used while she carried him, but her habit was not as bad as when she was pregnant with Michael. Todd has a learning disorder as well as severe hyper-activeness. Bianca fought to keep the brothers together, but it is hard because she already had three children. Because her sister works for children services, she was able to pull some strings to help her obtain the boys, and ten-year-old Nicky.

Just last month Nicky came to live with Bianca. Nicky's mother made her sleep with grown men in order to support her habit. Her first experience came when she was only seven years old. Nicky told Bianca that she's had sex with over thirty men for her mother. She was often beaten by the men or her mother when she refused to perform oral sex, or gang banging's. She finally had the courage to run away from home, but only to find herself homeless in the streets. There she was subjected to the same punishment. She sold her body for food, and slept in parks and abandoned and rat infested apartment buildings. Finally Nicky could take no more abuse. She took a piece of glass from a broken beer bottle and cut her wrists. Luckily she was discovered by a jogger in the park and was rushed to the hospital. After about two weeks of recovering she was placed with Bianca. While Nicky was still in the hospital, doctors discovered that she was infected with the AIDS virus. This was a concern for Bianca because of the well-being of the other children, but not enough to make her turn away from this troubled girl that needed her.

Dre was falling fast and hard for Bianca. For the first time in his life he was madly in love with a woman. Ever since the two of them had been dating, he has wanted to do nothing but be near her.

They've spent almost every night together, either at Bianca's or his place. Because of the children, most of their evenings were spent at her apartment, but Dre didn't mind as long as he was with her. He was also becoming attached to the children. Being their reminded him of when he was younger, trying to keep him and his sisters together. He felt Bianca's struggle for those children and he wanted to help her. He also felt a sense of guilt. He wondered if the very same drugs that he was putting on the street, were the same drugs that caused these babies pain and misfortune. He always knew he was part of poisoning the streets but he had never come face to face with the victims of his wrong doings. Dre wanted to make it up to those children in a bad way. He was constantly buying them clothes, bikes, toys...whatever he thought would bring a smile to their faces, and Bianca's. He immediately began assisting her with her rent and groceries to help ease the burden, but he felt that wasn't enough.

Dre also felt guilty because he knew he was not being totally honest with Bianca. Although he hadn't actually lied to her, he knew he was hiding who he really was. He knew that if she ever found out that he was a drug dealer that she would have nothing more to do with him, and she would hate him forever. He did not want to betray the trust that she was beginning to have for him. Dre knew that he wanted Bianca to love him as he felt he was starting to love her.

He was already beginning to neglect his duties with Angel. For instance, he canceled a meeting that he scheduled with Domino and T.J. so he could take Bianca and the kids on a trip to Disney World. He was ignoring pages from Angel or the guys for hours, if he returned them at all. He keeps his cellular phone turned off so he wouldn't be disturbed, or arouse suspicion from Bianca. Once Bianca thought that maybe he was talking to another woman on his phone because he left the room for privacy while he discussed something with T.J.

Bianca's plight to adopt the children legally did not look bright. Because of her financial situation and her unfavorable and inadequate living arrangements the state felt she could not properly accommodate them. She was told she had them temporarily until they could be placed in other, more suitable homes. She was distraught. She hated to see them bounced around from family to family. Plus, she had grown so attached to them, and she didn't trust anyone else to take care of them. She felt they needed special attention that only she could provide. Tim and her sister were doing everything they could to pull strings but so far nothing was working.

Late one night while everyone was asleep, Lindsey, the four year old, began to scream with terror. Dre and Bianca sprang to their fee and ran towards her bedroom. In the small room were a set of bunk beds and two cribs where the babies were sleeping. In one bed lay, a half-asleep Nicky, and the other, which belonged to Lindsey, was empty.

"Where is she," screamed Bianca, looking at Nicky for answers. "Lindsey honey, where are you? ...its mommy," she said while looking underneath the bed.

"I'll go look in the other rooms," said Dre.

"Dre, check the door, make sure it's locked. Oh God, what if she ran outside!"

"No, she's not out here, and the door is still locked," he yelled from the other room as he took another look around in the kitchen. "Lindsey, baby its okay, no one is going to hurt you, sweetie. Come out, you're scaring your mother to death."

"It's not funny, Dre. She has these nightmares all the time, poor baby," she said as she checked the closet once again. She pushed back the clothes, and looked in the corner. Underneath a pile of blankets was Lindsey. She was shaking profusely. Bianca reached down and pulled the frightened child out of the closet.

"No, noooo…don't let him get me pleeease…don't let him…he's going to hurt me again! I don't want to leave mommy," she cried uncontrollably. Bianca tried to calm her special little girl.

"Oh baby please don't cry. I don't want you to go away either, and I'm never going to let anybody hurt my precious little angel, don't your worry. Please stop crying, sweetie, it's okay," she said, holding and rocking the frantic child. Lindsey had dreams of her father abusing her all the time and she thinks he will take her away from Bianca. Dre stood back watching Bianca console the little girl. He felt so helpless. Then he looked at the other children that had gathered in the room. He cautiously moved closer to Bianca and reached his arms out for Lindsey.

"Hey Pumpkin…" Lindsey looked at him and then quickly put her face in Bianca's chest pulling away from Dre. She was still unsure about him, or any man for that matter. She was actually afraid for him to be near her. "I won't hurt you sweetheart, I love you, and I don't want you to have to go away either. I want you to stay here with me and mommy forever. Would you like that?" Lindsey slowly shook her head yes, but never looked up at him. Tears began to fill his eyes. He thought back to the fears he had not knowing when someone would take him or his sisters away from his home. He knelt down in front of them grabbing Bianca's hand.

"Lindsey, can I hug you so you won't be scared anymore?" She shook her head no. "Please, I love you, and I love mommy too," he said as he looked at Bianca and nodded his head yes. He had never actually said it to her before, even though he was feeling it for some time. Bianca looked at him in astonishment as her eyes continued to fill with tears. She too was in love with Dre, but she was afraid to tell him. She squeezed his hand and silently moved her lips to say, "I love you too."

"Honey do you feel a little better? You want mommy to lay here with you for a while," she asked. Lindsey shook her head yes while Dre wiped her runny nose with a tissue that he had gotten for Bianca.

"I'll wait for you in the other room baby," he whispered to Bianca as he kissed her goodnight. "Come on guys, let's get back to bed. Tell mommy goodnight," he said, as he motioned for the boys to leave out of the room.

"Goodnight mommy," they said in unison, as Todd helped his brother back to their room. Michael was able to scoot along on his little limbs very well.

"Night, night babies…I love you," said Bianca.

"Goodnight daddy," said a little voice coming from underneath Bianca. Dre turned around and looked at the little girl. He was so moved by Lindsey, and before he realized it she had jumped from the bed and hugged his legs. Bianca began to cry aloud as she watched Dre pick the little girl up.

"You don't know how happy you have made me pumpkin." He held her tight as Bianca stood and joined in the union. "I love all of you, so much," he said.

It wasn't long before Lindsey had fallen fast asleep. Bianca came into the bedroom where she found the smiling Dre.

"Did you hear what she called me," he asked, grinning from ear to ear.

"How could she not love you? You are the most sweet and gentle man in the world. She loves you, we all love you baby," she said as she laid down on top of him.

"Does mommy love me as much as I love mommy?"

"More," she said as she kissed his lips. She gave him the deepest kiss that she had ever given him. They could both feel the passion erupting between them. Even though they have been spending the night with each other, they had never made love. Bianca had never made love to any man. She was a virgin, but tonight, after 24 years of saving herself for the right man, she knew she had finally found him, and she wanted him. All these nights, Dre had been content with just holding her in his arms. He knew she was a virgin, and he thought that was just as special as she did, so he never tried to make any moves on her. Even tonight, it was obvious that she wanted to make love, but Dre stopped her. As bad as he wanted her, he had something else in mind, something even more special.

"Baby, if I could wait for these four weeks, and you all these years, what's a little while longer going to hurt? I want you so bad, and it's killing me not to make love to you but I want us to wait a little while longer."

"Home much longer Dre" I want you now. I feel as if it's the perfect time and you're the perfect man."

"Shhh," he whispered as he kissed her gently on her lips. "Trust me baby, just a little while longer."

The evening appears pretty calm a Terry walks pass three men shooting dice underneath a street light on the corner of a rough part of town. His clothes are dirty, far different from his usual extremely neat appearance. He suspiciously looks around as he approaches an old, seemingly abandoned, house. A younger but obviously drug addicted woman grabs his arm as he walks onto the porch. "Hey baby, can I go in there with you? I can make you feel good if you make me feel good," she slurs.

He looks at her with disgust, snatching his arm away as he enters the house. Inside drug addicts, young and old, sit all around the floors as they smoke crack. He approaches a young male sitting on a couch nearby as a woman is on her knees giving him oral sex. Terry waits patiently as she continues. He notices a small child in the corner, sitting next to her crack-smoking mother. Finally, the young girl that was pleasuring the drug dealer stood to her feet and wiped her mouth. The drug dealer hands her two crack rocks. She walks quickly to the side of the room hands a man one of the rocks and they begin to smoke together. Terry continues to appear disgusted then hands the dealer money in exchange for his own crack. He finds a spot on the floor and begins to smoke.

A NEW BEGINNING

The next few days Dre met with Tim to get all the details of Bianca's case. He had a few ideas but he needed to know all of his options first. Tim couldn't believe his ears when Dre told him of his plan to help Bianca.

"Man, I can't believe how hard you fell for this woman. Are you sure you know what you're doing my friend," Tim asked. Dre smiled and leaned back in his chair,

"Man, she is too good to be true. I don't think there's anything I wouldn't do for her and those kids. No. I don't just feel sorry for her, I'm in love with her. Laugh if you want to, I don't care. I think she is definitely the one."

Dre felt good when he left Tim's office. He couldn't wait to put his plan to work, but first he had to figure out how he was going to explain his disappearance this weekend. He had to fly to Venezuela to meet with Angel. He was pissed off at Dre because he has been unable to reach him, and he had not done certain things that he'd told him to do. Dre didn't want to start lying to Bianca, but he had no choice. He'd hope this would be the last time. He planned to let Angel know that he was ending his relationship with him no matter what. He planned to try and sell him on the idea of Domino taking over the operation. Even though Angel hated Domino, and his savage tactics, he had to admit that he wouldn't be a bad option.

Dre told Bianca that he had to go to Venezuela on business to close a deal for an associate. He thought he did an excellent job of smoke screening the truth, and it worked to his advantage that she didn't ask any questions. All she wanted to know was when her man was coming back home.

Saturdays are usually such long days for Bianca in the salon. Since she only worked Thursday through Saturday, her appointments piled up. She normally takes her first appointment around 7am, and she never gets out of there before 10pm. Since her and Dre had been seeing each other, he has helped her with the nanny expenses so she could afford to work longer hours and not have to worry about the kids.

By the time she arrived home all of the children were in bed except for Nicky, who was sitting alone in the dark living room.

"Hi sweetie, how was your day?" Nicky didn't respond. "Honey, are you alright?" she asked as she bent down in front of her. Still no sound came from her. Bianca sighed because she knew Nicky was worried about her condition, and she did not know what to do. What was she suppose to say, "Everything will be fine," when it's not. Nicky was dying, and that was an ugly truth that they were going to have to come to grips with.

"Can we talk about it," said Bianca, pulling Nicky closer. "I know you don't know me very well, and you may be very uncomfortable talking to me about something so personal, but I want you to know that I'm here for you anytime. No, I'm not your real mother, and I realize you probably miss her despite what she has done to you. I only pray that one day you will learn to trust and love me, as I love you. If you want to cry, we can cry together. If you want to scream, go ahead. If anger is what you're feeling, hit me, but please don't try to keep this inside and try to handle everything yourself, because this is bigger than you are sweetheart, and it can eat a whole in your soul."

Up until now Nicky sat very still and silent, staring at the floor. Suddenly, she jumped up and ran towards the door, screaming at Bianca, "Just leave me alone okay! I don't want to talk to you, I don't want to talk to the doctors, or nobody. I just want to hurry up and die."

"Wait, where are you going sweetheart, please let me help you." Bianca ran towards her but Nicky began fighting and kicking. Bianca realized that she had to calm her down, so she wrestled her to the floor, begging her to stop, but Nicky continued to try and break free.

"Why does God hate me," she cried aloud. "Bad things are always happening to me, people are mean to me, why…, what did I do, what did I do wrong?"

"Oh, Nicky, don't say that! God does love you, so much. Don't ever think that he is punishing you, you're just a baby," she said as she began rocking the crying little girl.

"Then why did he let my mother…and those men hurt me all the time like that?" Bianca could not answer her. She herself had often questioned why God would allow bad things to happen to innocent babies. Life seems so unfair, she thought. All she could do was cry and hold her tightly. She scrambled to find the right words to say to try and bring some kind of comfort to this child, but there was were none. She looked up towards the ceiling and raised her arms.

"Oh God, we need you now Lord. Please help this poor baby, cause she is hurting, and she needs to know you are there. She needs to...know you are real. Show us how to get through this Lord...because we don't know how," she cried. Bianca held the tiny framed little girl for hours. They cried and prayed together until the sun was beginning to peek through the blinds. Bianca had her hands full, and she knew things were only going to get worse, but she refused to give up. She was right where she wanted to be.

The next afternoon she received a message from Dre stating that he promised to be home on the next evening. She felt a sense of relief, because she needed his strength to help her get through. He told her that he had something special planned and to have Maggie come over to sit with the children. She was very excited and curious to know what he had up his sleeve.

It was almost six o'clock, and he called from the airport saying that he would pick her up by 7:30. Bianca was very nervous like it was their first date or something. It was probably the anticipation of him coming home after being gone for almost a week. She hoped that he didn't have to take extended business trips often, because she was beginning to get used to him always being there.

Nicky and Lindsey watched as she put on her makeup.

"You look so pretty mommy. Will I look like you when I get big?" asked Lindsey.

"Honey you are already very pretty. You look like a little doll." Lindsey enjoyed putting on Bianca's lipstick and playing grown up.

"See mommy, I'm pretty like you," she said as she smiled at Bianca.

"I know, you're such a big girl. You wanna get the brush and help me do my hair?" Lindsey reached for the hairbrush, but Nicky beat her to it. The two immediately started arguing over who was going to brush Bianca's hair. Suddenly the doorbell rang. Bianca yelled for Maggie to answer it.

"Was that Dre?" she asked as Maggie came into the bedroom.

"Well no, not exactly. It's a limo driver. Apparently Mr. Lanier has sent a car for you." Bianca's mouth flew open in amazement.

"You're kidding, right?" she said as she walked toward the door. The children ran behind her, "OOOH, a limousine," they sang. "Are you going in that mommy, are you rich?" Bianca laughed as she put on her coat, "No, I'm not rich. I wish I were though. She kissed all the children goodnight, and told Maggie that she wasn't sure what time she'd be back.

"Don't worry about a thing, have a good time, you deserve it. I'll stay here all night if you want me to, "Maggie smiled as she winked her eye at Bianca.

Bianca had never ridden in a limousine before so she was very excited. Suddenly she began to feel a little underdressed. She was wearing a blue silk dress, but she felt as though she needed something a little more classy and elegant. Obviously, Dre had planned a special dinner somewhere fancy, she thought.

"Could you wait a second please? I'll be back in three minutes," she asked the driver, as she hopped out of the car and ran into the house. The children sat on the couch anxiously waiting for her to come out. Finally she opened the door. She had changed into a stunning black sequined mini dress with spaghetti straps and sequined heels to match.

"Look at mommy ya'll, she looks like a princess," said Todd as he opened the door for her. The driver once again opened the rear door for Bianca. "You look lovely Miss Dupree, Mr. Lanier will be pleased.

"Why thank you very much. I think I'm finally ready to go now," she said as he closed the door. She was impressed with Dre's taste. He was definitely full of surprises and she loved that. She picked up the phone to speak to the driver, like she had seen done on television many times. "Excuse me, where are you taking me? Are we picking up Mr. Lanier also?"

"I'm sorry ma'am; I'm not supposed to say at Mr. Lanier's request. He told me to tell you to just sit back and enjoy the ride, and that he couldn't wait to see you.

The driver drove for nearly a half hour. She did not recognize the area at all. Every time he neared a nice restaurant she expected him to stop, but he kept passing them by. "Where could we be going? Maybe to a play or to some type of show, she thought" Soon they turned into a residential area. Now she was really confused. Maybe they were picking up another couple, and Dre was with them or something. The limo finally stopped in front of a beautiful two-story home with several large palm trees swaying in the yard. "This must be Tim's house," she thought. Since he was a lawyer, she expected him to own such a fabulous home. The driver walked around to the door and opened it.

She had a puzzled look on her face. "I'm getting out here?" she asked.

"Yes ma'am, Mr. Lanier is waiting for you inside. Come with me, I'll walk you to the door," he said as she grabbed his awaiting are and headed up the long walkway. She didn't see neither Dre's nor Tim's car in the driveway. As they approached the huge glass entrance, the driver let go of her arm.

"This is as far as I go. You are to go inside alone, he said as he turned and began to walk back towards the car. Bianca rang the bell, but the driver insisted that the door was unlocked and to just go inside.

"Just walk into someone's house?" she asked, now extremely apprehensive. "But I don't know these people." The driver motioned for her to open the door again.

"Hello, hello," she said as she slowly walked into the grand foyer. The house had little lighting and this really made her scared to go any further. "Dre are you here?" Just then she noticed rose petals on the marble floor leading down some steps and into another room. She slowly followed the trail into the dining room where she saw an amazing sight. The candlelit room was filled with dozens of bouquets of red roses and there had to have been over fifty balloons. "Oh my God what a beautiful sight," she thought.

"Pssst."

Quickly she turned towards the sound. There was her man standing in the doorway looking like brand new money.

"Hello my beautiful Bianca," he said as he pulled a single red rose from behind his back. Bianca smiled and trotted towards him. She threw her arms around his neck and kissed him feverously.

"Dre, what's going on, and who lives here." Ignoring her question he continued to kiss her lips to try to get her to stop talking.

"I missed you girl, and you look gorgeous in that dress."

"Dre, what do you have up your sleeve? Are we going to dinner or something? Tell me, what's the surprise…, and who lives here, Tim?" Dre looked down at his inquisitive girlfriend and smiled from ear to ear.

"You are worst than a kid at Christmas. Do you really wanna know what the surprise is?"

"Yes, tell me! What?"

"Go over to the balloons and pick one, anyone of them." Bianca quickly followed his instructions and picked out a balloon. She looked at Dre puzzled for more instructions. "Okay, pop it." Bianca looked at the balloon for a second then she began to squeeze until it popped.

"Whew." A small heart shaped piece of paper fell from it. She bent down and picked it up.

"Read it baby," said Dre. She looked at the paper and began to read it aloud.

"Bianca, will you marry me? I love you, Andre." Bianca looked at Dre with disbelief in her eyes. Then she read the note again to make sure it said what she thought it said. She couldn't speak. Dre began to walk toward her holding a small black velvet box.

"I love you Bianca Dupree, and I want to spend the rest of my life loving you, cherishing you and taking care of you," he slowly got down on one knee, "Please say you will be my wife, please say yes." She looked into his eyes and they were beginning to fill with tears. He opened the box and inside was the largest diamond ring she had ever seen. She gasped for breath as she covered her mouth. She was so overwhelmed by his sudden proposal.

"Oh baby, I'd be a fool if I didn't marry you. Yes, yes, yes! I love you," she said as he stood up and embraced her.

"Oh…I was so afraid that you would say no. I know we haven't known each other long, but I promise you I am so sure that God sent you here just for me." They hugged and kissed each other again, and again.

"Oh yea, I almost forgot. There's more to the surprise."

"Something else, what more could there possibly be," she asked.

Dre walked out the living room and stood at the foot of the stairs.

"Okay guys you can come out now," he screamed. From upstairs ran Nicky, Todd, Lindsey, and Maggie was carrying Michael.

"Surprise," they screamed. Bianca couldn't believe her eyes. They all ran up and grabbed her.

"Where did you guys come from, and how did you beat me here?" Didn't I leave you guys home and dressed for bed? Dre walked behind her and whispered in her ear,

"Welcome home honey." Bianca pulled away and stood back.

"Home?"

"Yes baby, this house belongs to you and the kids. Bought and paid for, so no one can ever take it from you. I was giving this to you whether you were going to marry me or not. Now you can provide a better home for them.

"Dre…Oh my God, Dre…I love you, I love, I love you! Did you hear that kids, this is our new home," she screamed as she jumped into his arms. The children ran and embraced the couple.

"We're a family now mommy, just like I prayed for," said Lindsey. Now we can stay together forever and no one will take us away from you." Bianca just smiled at the children. She hoped this house was the ticket for the adoptions to be approved. She did not want to get the kids hopes up too high by assuring them.

"Let's hope and pray that the judge will let us stay together," she said.

"Baby, I've already talked to the judge. He plays golf with my senior partner at the firm. I explained to him my intentions and he agreed to give you the children." Bianca couldn't hold back the tears anymore. All of her prayers had been answered. She looked at the faces of **HER children,** and for the first time they had a glow filled smile. Dre had made everything possible for them.

"Come on baby, let me show you around your new five bedroom home," said Dre. "Our five bedroom home," smiled Bianca.

The large house had huge bedrooms and four bathrooms, more than enough space for them. There was a large basement that could be used for storage and a recreation room where the kids could hang out. In the backyard, there was a large pool that the kids instantly approved of.

"Mommy can I have a swing set," asked Lindsey.

"Anything you want sweetheart," said Dre. "I'm going to install a basketball court for you Todd. I can teach you how to play like me. Oh yeah Maggie, there is an extra room for you if you're interested in a full-time live in position. How 'bout it, free room and board and a small salary? We could really use your help, and I know you are tired of sleeping on your sister's couch. You will have your own private bathroom and everything."

Maggie was speechless. She could not believe how generous this man was for them. She had only been in the states for four months and she had been helping Bianca out here and there. She was from Trinidad and didn't know too many people other than her few cousins, her sister and Bianca. Dre had made her an offer she could not refuse. "Oh bless you Mr. Lanier, bless your soul…Thank you so much," cried Maggie.

Dre looked at his family and smiled, "God has already truly blessed me."

THE NIGHT IS YOUNG

The evening was still young for Dre and Bianca. He still had plans for his beautiful fiancée. After the family celebrated for a while together, the limousine driver took Maggie and the children home. The kids were truly excited about the ride because none of them had ever been in a limousine before. The smiles on their faces were enough for Dre. He knew he was doing the right thing for them and felt good about it.

The couple had the house all to themselves now. They drank champagne in front of the fireplace, kissed and danced to soft jazz. Dre became lost in her eyes as they exchanged "I Love You's" and the softness of her voice carried him off to heaven. Deeper and deeper their kisses became as he slowly caressed her back. His 6'4" 200lb body cradled her petite frame down towards the white throw rug beneath her.

"Umm," she moaned, as she held on tight.

"Just relax baby, let me take care of you," Dre whispered softly in her ear. Slowly he stood before her in the shadows of the flame lit room, unbuttoning his shirt, but careful not to take his eyes off his queen. "Don't you move, I'll be right back,"

"Where are you going," she asked.

"You trust me don't you baby," he said as he came from the kitchen carrying a glass bowl filled with hot oil. She rose towards him as he reached behind her to free her from her dress. Bianca shook with anticipation as he kissed her neck and shoulders ever so slightly. "Lie on your stomach, I've got a treat for you," he said as he nibbled her earlobe. Bianca jumped with delight. Slowly he dripped the hot oil onto her back and watched it as it rolled down to her buttocks.

"Oh, that feels wonderful baby," she gasped. Dre admired her thin-bronzed body as it glistened from the oil. The light coming from the fireplace was just enough for him to see her curves.

"Bianca, you are so beautiful, baby," he said as he leaned forward and licked her down the center of her back, teasing her as he went lower, and lower until his tongue was parting her cheeks. Bianca shivered in ecstasy. "We've got all night, I'm in no hurry," said Dre as he turned her onto her back and gently kissed her breast. Bianca reached down and stroked his curly locks. His lips found her bellybutton and then her anxious wet mound. She gasped with relief because she had been waiting for him to kiss her between her thighs.

"Don't stop baby," she moaned, grabbing his head and pulling him into her. She lifted her hips off the rug to meet his juicy tongue. Faster and faster she moved until she screamed out in ecstasy. "Oh, baby, baby...yes...oh Dre...oh." Her body shook uncontrollably for a moment.

"Are you my baby," asked Dre with a boyish grin. He knew he had just rocked her world.

"Um...um," was all she could say. She laid there lifeless for about thirty seconds as he ran his fingers through her hair. "Okay, it's my turn," she said as she rolled over on top of him. Slowly she licked him from his toes to the insides of his thighs. Dre jumped with excitement, because he knew what was coming, but instead she began licking his chest, skipping his throbbing manhood completely. Dre realized she had never been with a man before so his chances of oral stimulation were slim. Bianca began to giggle because she knew she had gotten him good. "Like you said, I've got all night to enjoy you," she teased. Dre didn't like the reverse effect on him. He was much too horny and filled with anticipation for games. Finally Bianca licked her lips and lowered them around his awaiting penis. "Umm," she moaned, as she slowly moved up and down playing with him in her mouth with her tongue. Dre lifted his head off the floor so he could watch his penis disappear deep inside her throat. "You know exactly what I want don't you," she said looking at him with hungry eyes.

"Oh…I sure do baby, yes…I do, and I'm about to give it to you too," he said as his eyes began to roll around in the back of his head. "You want it baby…here it…comes…ba…by, uh…uh…shit," he screamed as he tried to pull away from her. He didn't want to overwhelm her with his hot juices on her first time, but surprising to him she held on to his throbbing meat, gulping every drop he had to give.

"Yum, yum…You taste as good as you look," she said as she gave him one last kiss. Dre just laid there with a dazed look on his face.

"My God…I haven't been inside you yet and I'm already sprung. That was so intense baby," he said trying to gasp for breath. "Girl I love you so much," he said pulling her down on top of him.

Throughout the night he was ever so gentle with her. They made love with endless passion and heat. Dre made Bianca's first night of lovemaking a magical moment filled with tenderness and emotion. As she drifted off to sleep with her head on his chest, she knew she had found her knight in shining armor and he was there to protect her forever.

Dre's Mercedes creeps slowly through the cemetery. He sighs as he parks along the curb, looking at Uncle Terry as he sits in front of Dre's parents and his grandmother's tombstones.

Terry sniffles as he stares blankly, while tracing his mother's name with his finger. His hair is long and uncombed and he has an equally unkempt beard.

"Aunt Carol said I'd probably find you here," says Dre from behind. Terry does not turn around. "Why haven't you returned any of my calls Unc?" Terry continues to ignore him. "Aunt Carol is worried sick about you, we all are." Terry snickers, "Is that right?"

Dre nervously prepares for his next question. "Are you using?"

Terry finally looks at him in disgust, "Are you selling?" Dre looks shocked.

"Are you the reason my mother is dead?" Terry cries! Dre is speechless while giving him a puzzled look.

Domino was enjoying Atlanta. He loved women and Atlanta was full of them, and full of strip clubs. He went to Magic City, a popular black club at least three nights a week. All the dancers knew him as the "Big Balla," meaning the one with all the cash, and he didn't mind spending it on them. Domino loved to show off, and every night he took at least two girls home for a private party. He was very flashy. He wore a lot of expensive jewelry loaded with diamonds such as a presidential Rolex watch, and a Mercedes Benz symbol made of diamonds around his neck. He drove a black, four door-600 Mercedes and a red Viper. No doubt about it, you knew him when you saw him, and you knew he was loaded. He was doing exactly what Dre had told him not to do, bringing attention to himself, but it was too late.

Already known for being a big drug dealer and a pimp in the city, he lived in an expensive high rise apartment in Buckhead, a very exclusive area in Atlanta. He was also secretly having a two-million dollar estate built on the outskirts of the city. He knew Dre would trip if he found out that he was spending money like that. The plan was to wait until they were out of the game before they spent large amounts of cash like that. Dre knew that large transactions would tip off IRS, and the Feds. But of course, Domino being hard headed and rebellious decided to do what he wanted to with his money. Since they expanded their operation, Domino was making close to $200,000 a month, and it was burning his pockets.

All the work had been completed on Domino's new home. He was meeting a contractor for some additional work that he needed done. He originally told the contractor that he wanted his basement finished for a recreation room, and then once he arrived, he changed his order. Domino wanted him to build a secret wall so he could hide drugs and money. He had over a million dollars in cash, and nowhere to hide it. He surely couldn't walk into the First National Bank with a couple of suit cases full of money. He needed something that no one knew about, especially the police, so just in case they came into his house, hopefully they would be able to find his stash.

"Looks good Eddie, and you finished quick too," said Domino, as he inspected the secret wall.

"Yeah, I told you it wouldn't take anymore than a few days," said Eddie as he continued to put his equipment away.

"How much do I owe you man," asked Domino as he opened his gold briefcase. "Ugh, let's say about $1500 for everything. I ain't trying to get rich too quick," he laughed.

"$1500 huh," laughed Domino, "No problem." Domino pulled a 9mm out of his briefcase. Eddie looked up and saw the gun pointed at his head. He fell to the floor in horror.

"Hey man, if that's too much…please, I'm an old man just trying to make a living for myself and my wife…Please, please, I don't want no trouble mister," he begged, as he held his hands up over his face as if he could shield the bullet. Domino looked down at the frightened old man with a glazed look in his eyes. Murder was no stranger to him. He actually got off on seeing people beg for their lives.

"I know what you mean man. I don't want no trouble either, and I certainly can't have you sneaking back in here later and stealing my money now can I? For a moment Eddie had a confused look on his face, then he realized what the wall was for.

"Oh no, you don't have to ever worry about me coming to steal anything. I'm a Christian man, and I don't take nothin' that ain't given to me," he cried, as he rapidly shook his head.

"So you say you're a church going man huh, Eddie?"

"Yes sir, me, and my wife don't miss a Sunday. I'm a deacon in my church and everything."

"Well I think it's time you started praying, cause you about to go see your maker," said Domino as he pulled the trigger and put two bullets in that poor old man's face.

Domino drove Eddie's truck and his lifeless body about thirty miles east of his house. Once he found a secluded spot, he set the truck on fire with the body inside of it.

"Hello," answered T.J.

"Hey baby. I thought you were coming home this weekend, what happened? I miss you so much. I can't stand this separation," said DeeDee.

"I'm sorry baby, I couldn't get away. Since your brother met some chick down there, I've been busy doing what he should be doing. I know you miss me baby, and I miss you too, but we have to be patient."

"T.J. I love a brother to death, but I am tired of putting my life on hold to satisfy him. I'm coming up there to be with you. I want to get married like we've planned T.J., I'm sick of waiting. I want you to be my husband. I want a baby, a home…Every year we promise the next year will be different. All we do is make empty promises to each other, and for what?"

"No more promises baby. Let's just do it."

"What? What do you mean?" asked DeeDee.

"I mean, February 14th is good for me, is it good for you?"

"To get married," she screamed.

"No silly, to have a garage sale. What else: I love you girl and it's time we made a commitment to our relationship. Dre swears we will be finish dealing with that crazy ass Colombian in about three months or less so everything should be cool by then." DeeDee was so excited. They had always talked about getting married, but never actually had a date set. T.J. was starting to realize that his devotion to his best friend could cost him DeeDee.

"We're finally almost there baby; I can feel it this time. Don't play with my emotions T.J., I'm serious as a heart attack."

"Me too…Hey baby, I gotta go. When is your next day off?"

"…Wednesday, Thursday, and Friday."

"I need to see you girl. I'm going to Western Union right now and wire you some money for a plane ticket so you can bring your fine ass here. When we hang up, call and make your reservations, then leave the information on my answering machine."

"Oh, I can't wait to feel you in my arms," moaned DeeDee.

"Oh yeah…Well I can't wait to feel something else," laughed T.J.

"Is that why you miss me? Dog boy, do you think of anything else?"

Dre had everything he always wanted. His life was finally beginning to come together now, except for his situation with Angel. His trip to Venezuela was a complete disappointment for him. Angel's constant promises of surrendering him from his claws, has now turned into threats. Angel seemed to be tightening his grip around Dre's neck instead of preparing to let him go. He told Dre that he would let him know when he was finished with him and for him not to ask him again. Angel believes that since he was responsible for Dre becoming a millionaire that he owed him his loyalty. Dre did all he could do to keep from swinging on Angel. He realized if he tried physically to persuade him that he would not make it out of the country alive. Angel had him by his balls, and this made him feel so vulnerable. How was he to begin a life with Bianca filled with lies?

Angel made sure he let Dre know he was unhappy about his relationship with Bianca. He told him that he was not as focused as he used to be and his new girlfriend was the problem. Angel went as far as to suggest to Dre that he should end his involvement with her. Of course Dre told him to go to hell and if he thought he could control his love life he was mistaken.

He also shot down Dre's idea of allowing Domino to run his operation. Angel reminded him of how he didn't trust Domino and how his flamboyant ways were bringing attention to the organization. Dre didn't dare mention T.J., because he knew T.J. wasn't interested in working past Dre's control. He was just as anxious to wash his hands of this life as Dre was.

It was about 4:30 in the morning when Dre got the call. It was T.J. mumbling something about Domino having been arrested that night for murder. Dre was still half-asleep but he knew what he heard. The phone also woke Bianca,

"Who is it honey," she asked, staring to see the clock on the nightstand.

"I'm sorry baby, go back to sleep; I'll take this in the other room." Dre sprung to his feet, put on his robe and went downstairs to continue his conversation. "T.J., what the hell is going on now man, and who, one of those niggas that was beefing about Southwest Atlanta?"

"Look, all I know is I was in Atlanta at his crib, you know, we were just chilling with a few girls and drinking a little bit, when all of the sudden cops were at the door."

"What! Don't tell me he had some shit on him," Dre said as he was becoming more and more irritated. He was convinced Domino had done something stupid.

"Naw, I don't think so, at least the cops didn't say anything about any drugs, they just cuffed him and took him to jail about thirty-minutes ago."

"I'm going to catch the first flight out in the morning. Keep your pager close, I'm going to need you to pick me up from Hartsfield airport. Oh yeah, what's the deal with his bail?"

"It's too soon, they haven't set it yet," T.J. said.

"Boy, that nigga stay in some shit. I knew it was time to tighten up on his ass," said Dre.

"Hey man, did you know about his crib?"

"His high-rise in Buckhead?" asked Dre.

"Naw...his new crib, Taj Mahal type shit," explained T.J. Dre threw his head back on the rear of the chair and sighed loudly in disgust, "Look man, like I said, I'll be there as soon as I can in the morning. You can fill me in on everything then," said Dre as he hung up the phone.

Dre headed back upstairs to his groggy fiancée, "Baby, is everything alright?" asked Bianca, as she sat up in the bed and turned on the lamp on the nightstand. Dre sighed as he sat on the edge of the bed.

"No, everything is not alright. Remember my friend in Atlanta that I've been telling you about...well he was arrested tonight for murder, and

I have to go and see what's up," he said, as he picked up the phone to make his reservations.

"Oh my God, Dre, murder? Are you planning to represent him?" Dre had no intentions of getting involved in Domino's case. It would only bring attention to their friendship, and plus there is no telling what they had on him. Dre needed to find out every detail involving this case for his own safety. He assured Bianca that he would only be gone for a couple of days, back in plenty of time to decide on a date and pick out their invitations.

T.J. met Dre at the baggage claim as planned. He could tell by the look on Dre's face that he was stressed out.

"What's up man, I'm parked right up front, where's your bags," T.J. asked with apprehension. He'd seen Dre like this before and he was just glad that he hadn't done anything.

"No, this is all I brought," he said holding a small leather like gym bag. He had only planned to be there for that day, long enough to make Domino's bail, if he had one, and find out what was going on. First he wanted T.J. to take him by Domino's new house. He was extremely pissed about that because he gave specific instructions about not making large purchases. He had all of Domino's keys so he was able to show Dre the entire house. Just as T.J. had described, it was indeed grand. Domino has an indoor pool with a waterfall and bar, marble throughout the house, and a master bedroom almost the size of Dre's entire house. Yeah, Domino had definitely crossed the line this time. Dre was determined to get Domino out of his life before he caused him trouble, if it wasn't already too late.

Once they arrived at the jail Dre immediately began gathering information about Domino's case and posted his bail. The buzzer sounded, the door opened, and out walked Domino. He was still furious about his arrest.

"Man this is bullshit Dre," he immediately began trying to plead his case. He knew when he saw Dre there in Atlanta that he had major explaining to do. Dre didn't open his mouth, and his silence ripped through Domino like a blade. The trio didn't say anything until they got into the car. Dre was the first to break his silence.

"Head out to the crib man," he said to T.J. as they started out in traffic. He sat up front with T.J. while Domino sat in the back. Without turning around he said his first words to Domino,

"You know, I stuck my neck out on the line for you, man…and it seems like I'm constantly covering up your fuck ups."

"My fuck ups," Domino blurted out with an attitude.

"Close your damn mouth for once! That's been your damn problem, you don't listen to anyone," yelled Dre as he turned around in his seat as if he were about to swing at Domino.

"You have to always do things your way...the wrong way. You are so fucking stupid man! What were you thinking about when you killed that old man Domino?"

He didn't even bother to ask Domino whether he had done it or not, because he knew that he was capable and it was right up his alley. Apparently the contractor Domino shot had made a call on his cell phone telling his wife that he had finished his job and was on his way home. Also, Domino's address and phone number was written down in his appointment book at home.

"You've really fucked up this time," T.J. said as he shook his head. He had been quiet up until then. Domino was beginning to feel picked on by his so-called friends.

"Don't act like ya'll are so damn righteous. Ya'll are just as illegal as I am, so don't judge me. As far as I'm concerned, we are all in this together. I'm going to tell you like this Dre, if you don't figure out a way to get me out of this shit, we are all going down," Domino stated in a cocky voice.

Dre and T.J. looked at each other in disbelief. What does his stupidity have to do with their drug operation? Dre slowly turned and looked at his lifelong buddy. He didn't want to fly off the handle because he realized Domino was probably speaking out of anxiety.

"Excuse me," Dre said. T.J. kept his eye on Domino in the rear view mirror. "This nigga done lost his mutha fuckin' mind," Dre thought to himself. Domino showed no fear towards Dre.

"That's right nigga, you heard what I said. I don't know what you have to do, or who you have to call, maybe one of your big shot lawyer or judge friends …I don't know. Just handle yo'business," he sarcastically said. "Anyway, they don't have no proof." "They can't put this on me and you're going to make sure of it too."

"Is that right?" Dre says quietly.

"You damn right," screamed Domino, "You remember what happened the last time you tried to leave me hanging? I liked your grandmother too."

Dre and Domino stared into each other's eyes. Dre could not believe what his "so called" friend was implying.

"You're a punk man," said T.J. "I can't believe you would sell out your homeboys because you made a fucked up decision."

"Turn around T.J., and take me to the airport," Dre said after he had been silent for a while. T.J. turned and looked at him with frustration. He knew Domino had pushed Dre's buttons and he didn't want them to fall out because of Domino's arrogance. T.J. has always been the mediator between the two. "My business is finished here. I came to help my friend, but he appears to have everything under control."

"Hey, we're in this together man, don't forget, as he leaned forward towards Dre. Dre chuckled aloud, "No…you're wrong, I'm not in this…and you my friend, need a good lawyer." Dre grabbed his bag from the trunk and T.J. walked inside the airport with him.

"Don't forget what I said Dre," Domino yelled from the car. "I'll call you tomorrow." Dre didn't even turn around.

"Hey man, you don't think he's serious do you?" asked T.J. "And what did he mean about your grandmother, you don't think he had anything to do with her death do you?" Dre ignored his question as he paid for his ticket.

"Look, take him home, and page me from a pay phone in four hours," said Dre as he walked toward the terminal.

The next morning, Dre ignored Domino's pages. It crushed Dre to know that the man he had grown to love as a brother would betray him as arrogantly as he was. He could think about the many times he had taken up for him. He now realized Angel had been right about him all along. Dre had to be in court early that morning but he had to stop by his office to pick up some files he'd forgotten. Just then his phone rang.

"Andre Lanier speaking, may I help you please?"

"Dre, why haven't you returned my pages man?" said Domino. Dre sat down in his chair,

"What do you want Domino? I am very busy this morning, plus I can't imagine what you have to say to me. Are you calling to threaten me again?" Domino had apparently been drinking the night before and was still pretty drunk.

"Hey man, you know I got much respect for you right? I don't know what's gotten in to me lately, sometimes I do and say some wild shit man. You do know that I would never rat on you don't you man, not with everything you've done for me all these years," Domino was beginning to cry as he was trying to explain himself to his best friend. "And you know I didn't mean what I said about your grandmother right?" Dre closed his eyes tightly as if he were trying to block out Domino's voice.

"Why are you telling me this," asked Dre. There was a long silence over the phone except for a few sniffles from Domino.

"I'm telling you this …because I need you to know …that you can trust me Dre. I'm your brother man and…I wouldn't hurt you…I love you…I love you Dre. Dre tried to fight back the tears, but the emotion as too strong for him. Domino realized he had hurt his friend deeply and didn't want to push him.

"Look man, I know you're busy. You can call me later if you want to I'm about to leave now, I have an appointment with a lawyer this morning, but I'll be back around noon.

"Domino wait!" Dre sprung to his feet, his pulse was racing, but he couldn't turn back now.

"Yeah man, what's up," asked Domino. Dre clenched the phone cord and put his head in his hands. After a long pause Dre slowly said,

"I…love you too…man." He slowly hung up the phone. He felt sick to his stomach. He hadn't planned to speak with Domino this morning and it caught him totally off guard. Dre ran down the hall past his secretary's desk and into the bathroom. He slid down in front of the toilet and threw his head into it. After he finished throwing up his breakfast, he stood up and looked at himself in the mirror. He could not keep the tears from coming.

"I'm the monster I never wanted to be," he thought. He washed his face trying to get himself together and left for the courthouse.

Domino grabbed his black suit jacket from the bed. He had already called his attorney to let him know that he was running late for his appointment. He was very nervous about his meeting. He had no idea what he was up against or the amount of evidence that was building up.

Domino patted his pockets and looked on the counter for his keys. He couldn't remember exactly where he put them when he came in because he'd gotten pretty wasted. As he opened his front door to check to see if he'd locked them in the car he heard a jingle. There they were sticking out of the lock on the door. Domino laughed at himself and said, "Damn man, you'd better be more careful, there are some crazy and dangerous people in this world." He then locked the door, walked down to the end of the driveway to his car. His sprinkler system was about to kick on so he tried to hurry up and jump into his car, accidently dropping his keys between the seats of his new Jaguar.

"Today just ain't your day D," he said as he started the ignition.

"KA BOOM, BOOM!" His car exploded with a powerful blast. A neighbor that was jogging past his house was knocked down by the eruption.

"Oh my God, somebody please help that man," she screamed. Domino's car was now scattered flames of metal all over his yard and into the street. Many of his neighbors and passer-by's ran towards his house to give their assistance.

"Oh shit he's a mess, don't look in there it's not a pretty sight," said an onlooker.

"Did anyone call 911," screamed a frantic voice from the crowd. Panic and fear engulfed the exclusive neighborhood of only about ten homes. Domino's home had only been complete for about two weeks and no one had actually seen or met him yet.

Finally sirens could be heard in the distance. The car was still burning when the fire trucks and police cars arrived. The police immediately roped off the area and attempted to control the growing crowd of people.

"He's crispier than a bucket of chicken," joked one of the police officers.

Once the flames were put out, the coroner attempted to remove what was left of Domino. His head had been blown through the back rear window; one of his hands was singed to the steering wheel, while the other arm was lying on the ground.

"There's not much left of this guy. Someone definitely wanted to get their point across," said the coroner, as he placed Domino's arm in a plastic bag.

"Come on people let's move it, there's not much to see here…you're blocking traffic," said Officer Graves as he continued to try to direct the flow of cars. A dark green BMW with dark tinted windows idly drove in front of the house. The driver window slowly came down.

"Excuse me officer, is that guy going to be alright?" T.J. asked.

"Not a chance, he's been blown to bits," the officer said as he waved T.J.'s car on through. T.J. looked at the car and watched as they removed Domino's body and placed it in the body bag.

"It didn't have to end this way my brother…rest in peace," said T.J. as he felt his eyes begin to tear. As instructed he picked up his cell phone, dialed Dre's pager number, and entered the code "187," which means murder.

THE LAST STRAW

Solemn music plays as "crackheads" walk up and down quiet the quiet street. Inside of the crackhouse, the scene is the same, babies crying, a couple fighting over a crackpipe as dozens of lost souls sit along the walls amongst trash, dirty needles and used pipes.

A young girl carrying a crying infant slowly moves through the crowd begging for hits of crack. Everyone ignores her. "Excuse me, can I get a hit she whispers" to a man sitting alone in the dark corner. "Hey" she says as she taps his foot, kneeling down closer. She gasps as she sees his face. It's Terry! His eyes are open and foam is oozing from his lips. A needle is stuck in his arm.

Over the course of the next few days Dre's feelings of suffocation grew even stronger. Between his beloved uncle's overdosing and ordering the death of his best friend, then actually following through with it, has taken its toll on him. The guilt in his heart was so heavy he often felt as though he could not go on.

Domino's memorial was a little more than he could stand. He and T.J. had to force themselves to go so no one would be suspicious. Dre actually turned around and headed for home three times, then once he finally reached the chapel he circled it for about an hour. By the time he walked through the church doors the service was almost over. The church was full of Domino's friends and family, many of which Dre knew as well. It was especially hard for him to face Domino's mother. Ms. Sharpe had made a complete turnaround since they were boys. She'd kicked her drug habit and was very active in the church and her community. She had almost become like a second mother to Dre. All in all, Dre kept his composure well until he looked over at Camille and Trent, Domino's long time girlfriend and their eighteen-month old son. Dre and T.J. were Trent's godfathers. Dre loved that boy as if he was his own son. When Trent saw him he wiggled and squirmed until his mother put him down. He looked like a little man wearing his white tuxedo with a little black bowtie and cummerbund. He tried to run towards Dre so he could pick him up but Dre quickly walked towards Domino's casket. He couldn't bear to hold that precious little boy knowing that he'd executed his father. As Dre drew nearer to his friends casket he felt the eyes of everyone in the church upon him but he didn't care. He slowly reached out and touched the closed box that held the one man that he'd gladly exchange places with. Tears raced down his face as he tried to conceal his emotions. Suddenly he gave out a choking sound and fell to his knees.

T.J. quickly reached down and grabbed Dre off the ground for fear of what he might blurt out next. Dre opened his eyes and saw it was his friend, "Look what we did man, he whispered."

"He's...gone," he cried as T.J. walked him to his seat.

This was the last straw for Dre. Drugs have brought him and his family nothing but pain and grief. It had to end and it had to end now. Angel's threats no longer hung over his head as they once did. The death of Uncle Terry, his best friend, Sterling, and the love he has for his fiancée and his new family gave him the strength he needed to challenge Angel. He now realized that no matter how many millions he made for Angel, it would never be enough. He would continue to use him until he quit or until Angel killed him.

Angel trusted no one so whether he quit today or ten years from now Dre knew he would be assassinated. Dre flew to Alabama and held a meeting with T.J. to begin making preparations to end the organization. Of course T.J. was more than ready finally to stop. They figured it would take at least another two weeks to pull their investments out smoothly and sever their ties. They would connect their dealers in Atlanta that once dealt with Domino, with the dealers in Alabama that dealt with T.J. Dre would then connect them with a Cuban in the Florida Keys that he had come to know through an associate in the firm that had once represented him in a drug case. Dre was already aware that Angel would not be pleased. He had always been against outsiders and people he didn't know, but Dre was determined to present his proposal and Angel could take it or leave it.

DeeDee however, had a better plan. She proposed Dre set up Angel in a DEA sting. Currently the bureau has limited information about Angel Sanchez and his cartel, so they would jump at the chance to finally get something solid on him. The only thing they had to figure out was how they would lure him without incriminating Dre & T.J. All of these years he had successfully kept his name and face out of the Feds files. DeeDee was sure they could devise a plan if not to arrest Angel, at least to make him believe agents were closing in on Dre and his operation, therefore he would be more trouble than he was worth. However, Dre was stubborn and impatient. He did not want to associate with Angel another day. After he and T.J.

has successfully merged the southeastern operation, he made his fatal call. As planned, he informed Angel of his merger and the change of command, and as he expected he disapproved.

"You insist on doing things your way don't you Dre? I'm running this operation, or have you forgotten that," said Angel as smug as he could. Dre chuckled aloud despite the lump in his stomach.

"This is not up for discussion Angel. Now I've set things up so there would not be a break in the flow of revenue for you." Angel interrupted him with a forceful voice,

"You've set it up, set it up my ass! You couldn't handle Domino, but let you tell it, you had that under control, right?" Dre was stunned. He had not told Angel about Domino's murder charge nor his death.

"Oh yeah, I know about that. If you hadn't killed him, I would have…along with you."

"Look, I've tried for many years to do this the way you wanted, but I'm tired of playing by your rules. As far as I'm concerned, it's your move. I've told you my plans, so I guess you have to do what you have to do," said Dre. He was about to shit in his pants but he had to stand firm and show no fear.

"It's that bitch isn't it?"

"What?" said Dre angrily.

"She put you up to this right?"

"Leave her out of this; she's blind to the whole situation. Look this is between you and I. You don't need me, you're going to make millions with or without me," he said as he hung up the phone. He knew this would piss him off but he had to show him he meant business. His palms were sweaty and his pulse was racing. He knew he was doing the right thing, he just prayed that God would help him through it. He knew the kind of man Angel was and he didn't think for one minute it was over. He knew he had not heard the last from Angel Sanchez.

POINT OF NO RETURN

DeeDee stood in the bathroom and stared at the home pregnancy test. She could not believe that after all this time was carrying T.J.'s child. Everything was finally starting to come together for her. T.J. was making plans to return to Miami in a couple of months for good. They were going to finally announce their engagement to Dre and the world. She prayed that he would give his blessings to her and his best friend and not feel as though he had been betrayed. Maybe they could have a double ceremony with him and Bianca she thought to herself.

"We are finally going to be a little family," she said aloud as she rubbed her tiny belly that cradled her and her lover's baby. She giggled to herself as she stared in the mirror imagining how fat she was going to get. She could hardly wait to tell T.J. the good news. "He's going to be so proud," she thought as she leaped across her bed towards the phone on the nightstand. "Where are you baby," she said as the phone rang continuously. "Hum, that's strange," she thought. He's usually home, still asleep this early in the morning. No problem she thought, "I'll just page him, and he'd better have an explanation as to where he is at 7:30 in the morning." He never called. For three day, she called and called, but no answer. Dre got the same results. He was also trying to reach his buddy with no success. This was definitely out of character for T.J. He knew that Dre did not like it when he didn't return his pages immediately, and he never went a day without, at least, putting his "I Love You" code in DeeDee's pager. She was beginning to worry, and for the first time she was suspicious of another woman.

Finally after a week, she received a message from him on her machine. "DeeDee, I'm sorry it has to end this way. I will always love you no matter what." She could hardly believe her ears. What prompted this change of attitude? Their last conversation was great. They were making wedding plans for the summer and he was just as excited as she was. They hadn't had a fight or even a small disagreement in a long time. Teary eyed and confused, she dialed his number in a panic. Still no answer.

"I don't believe this shit! There must be another bitch and if that's the case, he's not going to just leave some message on my damn machine," she uttered as she slammed the phone down. She was dumbfounded. Throwing her face into her pillow, she burst into a mad stream of tears. She could not understand why he would desert her like this. They'd always been able to talk and discuss problems within their relationship. She loved this man since she was 10 years old; he was her first and only lover.

What was she to do? He hadn't been home in days, or at least he wasn't answering his phone. She wanted an explanation from him. She wanted to tell him about their baby, hoping he would see his mistake. He needed to know that she was going to have his baby with or without him. She planned to see him face to face, today. She would fly to Alabama tonight, after her "Sanchez sting" briefing. He would have to tell her in person that he did not love her, did not need her as much as she needed him.

Bianca finished her last appointment early, so she hurried home to begin a romantic evening for her and her sweetie. Maggie had taken the children out for pizza and skating so the house was quiet for a change. Taking advantage of her serenity, Bianca decided to run a hot bath to unwind before she began dinner. The steam from the water put her in a hypnotic state as she laid her head back against the tub. She softly began humming to the song she heard playing in the background.

"Auh," she moaned. Bianca loved her new Jacuzzi tub. It was actually her favorite feature of her new home. As she lay with her eyes closed she could smell the beautiful jasmine oil that she had placed into her bath.

"You are beautiful," said an unfamiliar voice. Startled by the dark figure standing over her, Bianca screamed. "Oh my God, who are you? What are you doing here," shouted the terrified Bianca as she sprang out of the water and desperately reaching out for a towel that was lying near the tub. It was Angel Sanchez and he was holding a knife. He quickly grabbed the naked and shaking woman and covered her mouth with his hand as he placed the knife to her throat with the other.

"Don't make me kill you bitch," he whispered in her ear while throwing her wet body upon the vanity. Sheer terror filled her heart as he slammed her head into the mirror. The broken glass sliced her thighs and back as she squirmed beneath him. He placed the knife on her breast and slowly began to glide the sharp point, piercing her skin. A slow stream of dark blood rolled down her stomach.

As Bianca stared into the eyes of this monster standing before her she could feel her heart pounding through her exposed chest. She knew he was there to hurt her but she didn't know why. Glancing at her assailant she couldn't help but to notice his expensive watch, his neatly trimmed hair, and mustache. He was obviously not a robber in search of money. Bianca cringed as he slowly began to rub her inner thigh.

"Please, don't do this," she cried as he began to violate her.

"Shhhh!" You can thank your boyfriend for this one," he said as he began to slap her repeatedly in her face. She screamed after each blow while trying to defend herself, but the small framed woman was no match for his strength. She thought if she stopped resisting him that he would stop beating her but he continued. He held hr frail bloody body down on the counter top by her throat as he unbuckled his pants with his free hand. She began to cry because she knew her fate.

"No, no please," she wailed, as he forced her legs apart with his and rammed himself inside of her. "Oh, please, somebody help me," she screamed, as he punched her in her mouth. Blood spurt from her swollen lips.

"No, no," she whimpered, closing her eyes, praying he would stop, but once he did, she feared what he would do next. Angel backed up and stared down at the bloody Bianca, as he pulled his pants up.

"Dre was right, you do have a good piece of ass," he smiled, as he looked at himself in the shattered mirror and adjusted his hair. Bianca, too terrified to move, wept silently as she lay upon the broken glass, almost lifeless. Angel leaned down towards her and gently kissed her cheek. "You're not upset with me are you Bianca," he said as he winked his eye at her and disappeared through the bathroom door. Still afraid to move, because she didn't know whether he had left the house or was rummaging for money, Bianca could think of nothing else but the horrible things that Angel said to her.

"Dre knows him. He knew my name," she thought, as she attempted to lift herself from the counter. Some of the glass was lodged so deep into her skin that she let out a sharp wail. "Oh God…Please help me," she whispered, as she heard a door close down the hall. She found just enough strength to drag herself across the floor to a nearby closet. "My God, he's coming back to kill me!" Bianca feverishly attempted to hide herself behind some clothes. She could hear the thumping of her racing heart from beneath her chest as she heard the footsteps getting closer.

"Bianca, where are you honey?" It was Dre. Instead of being relieved at the sound of his voice, she felt horrified. All those evil things the stranger said to her played repeatedly in her head. Who was the man that she had come to love and trust? What was his relationship with the animal that had hurt her so bad, and was Dre going to hurt her too? Scared and shaking, she scrambled to hide deeper in the closet from the approaching voice. Dre heard the rustling in the closet and cautiously approached the door. He peered through the dark space and caught a glimpse of the quivering shadow. He quickly turned on the light. There in the corner, battered and bloody was his world.

"My God baby," he cried, as he rushed towards her. Bianca pulled away from him in fear.

"You're bleeding so bad! Please let me help you baby," he shouted in a panicked voice. Bianca stared right through him.

"No," she shouted, as she snatched her arm from him.

"It's okay baby, it's me, Dre. Who did this to you? Please, let me help you" he said, as the sight of the woman he loved made him cry. Her jet-black hair, still wet from the bath clung to her beaten body. Naked and cold, Bianca trembled as she finally broke her silence.

"Who are you?"

"Who...baby it's me," he said hesitantly coming closer to her.

"Don't touch me!" Confused, but cautious not to spook her anymore, Dre tearfully sat down near her. He could see the bruises on her body, but not the ones in her heart. "He said he knew you," she murmured, as tears continued to fall from her swollen eyes.

"Knew me?"

"He said...he said, it's your fault he did this to me," she shouted, as she began hitting him. Dre tried to comfort her but she continued frantically to attack him. "I hate you! I hate you Andre," she screamed, as he was finally able to grab her arms and hold her until she calmed down.

"Baby ...you don't know what you're saying. You don't mean that! I don't know who did this to ..." Dre froze. All he could do is shake his head in disbelief. It couldn't be Angel, he thought to himself. Would he resort to hurting the woman he loved just to prove a point? He knew it was time to come clean to her. Things were out of control and they had been for a long time. Dre slowly began to tell her the story of his life leaving no stone unturned. He told her about Sterling and his relationship with the man who had raped her. He begged her to understand how he had gotten himself and his family tangled into this dangerous web. "He hurt you to get back at me," Dre cried, as he leaned forward to bury his head into her breast. "Please don't leave me baby. I love you so much. I wouldn't do anything to hurt you or the children Bianca, you know that," he explained. Bianca slowly placed her trembling hand upon his head which was still resting on her breast. He broke down as he felt hr warmth again. The warmth that he thought he had lost forever.

DeeDee rehearsed what she would say all the way from the airport to T.J.'s house. She asked the cab driver to wait until she was sure he was home. After ringing his doorbell and walking around the house looking through windows, she finally spoke to a neighbor that was standing in his yard with his children. He told her that T.J. was very sick and was admitted into the hospital a few days earlier. DeeDee raced to the hospital in search of her lover but she was not prepared for what she was about to learn.

While she was inquiring at the nurse's station about him, one of his doctors happened to be standing nearby reviewing his charts. She was becoming hysterical because she had no idea why he had been admitted, and no one was willing to give her any information because she was not related to him.

"Excuse me. I'm Dr. Rhinehart and I'm one of Torez's physicians here at the hospital, maybe I can assist you," he said as he led her into a waiting area.

"Thank you doctor…I'm his fiancée and I'm here from out of town, and a neighbor told me that he was here. Please tell me what happened. What is going on? The doctor had a puzzled look on his face.

"You don't know about his condition?" DeeDee shook her head waiting anxiously for his response. "Torez has a very serious case of pneumonia," he said. DeeDee stared into his eyes looking for more.

"How serious," she stuttered. Dr. Rhinehart took a deep breath and sighed. She could tell he was very nervous and there was a lot more. He grabbed her hand. "His left lung has collapsed and his right one is very weak."

"What are you saying," Are you trying to tell me that he's dying doctor," she said wearily. He slowly nodded his head. Without looking up at her he added,

"I also ran a few more tests…he has AIDS," he said hesitantly. DeeDee stood up and snatched her hand away from him. "I'm sorry Miss Snipes, but he is dying." She felt as if the wind had been knocked out of her. She could not speak as bad as she was trying. She kept waiting for him to say that maybe he had confused T.J. with another one of his patients, but he never did. Feeling very weak, she sat back down on the couch; she could not seem to catch her breath. Tears raced from her eyes, yet she couldn't make a sound. The doctor ran over to the water cooler and poured her a cup. DeeDee slapped the cup of water from his hand and let out a scream.

"Nooooo. This can't be…See you don't understand doctor…we're getting married, and…and…and…oh my God…oh my God…we're having a baby," she cried as she gently placed her hands on her belly. "He doesn't even know he's going to be a father. T.J., oh baby…no, no, no," she screamed, as she jumped to her feet and started running down the hall. Dr. Rhinehart took off after her.

"Please Miss Snipes…wait. Nurse I need help over here!" She opened one room door, but he wasn't there.

"T.J.," she screamed.

"Ma'am, you can't go in there, ma'am," said a nurse who was walking another patient to his room. Dr. Rhinehart quickly grabbed her as the other nurses helped to restrain her.

"Please, I just want to see him! Why can't I see him," she cried.

"Miss Snipes, you must calm down. I will take you to him, but you have to get a hold of yourself. I want to help you," promised the doctor. DeeDee needed to sit down for a moment and get herself together before she was ready to see him. The doctor explained to her that he was very weak.

When she walked into the intensive care unit and saw him lying there lifeless, hooked up to a respirator, she knew she would not make it. She stood in the doorway for what seemed like forever, unable to move towards him. Her body felt limp, and just as she was about to turn around and run out of the room she heard a voice,

"It's okay, I'll go in with you." It was Dr. Rhinehart. He took her hand and led her towards the bed. Her feet felt heavy as if she were in quicksand and she pulled back many time, but he encouraged her to keep going.

"Oh sweetheart," she whispered, as she finally reached his side. She softly brushed her fingers through his hair and gently kissed his lips. She lowered herself onto a chair beside his bed, not taking her eyes off him for a second. Slowly he began to open his eyes. "Baby, I'm here," she said softly, as she started to cry. "You will do just about anything to keep from marrying me won't you," she smiled, as she pulled his hand up towards her face. Tears were beginning to roll down his face. He could hear and understand her well, but could not speak. Finally she could hold it no longer. "Why T.J.? How could you do this to us…to our baby? Please, don't leave us all alone, we need you so much," she cried as she buried her face into his chest. His eyes bulged at the news of his baby. He tried hard to communicate with her but he could only squeeze her hand. "Don't try to talk honey, I know you love me and I love you. I know we can get through this together…we have to. T.J. squeezed her hand once more as he gazed into her eyes.

He was dying and he was afraid. For the next few hours she tried comforting him so that he could relax and let go, but his eyes told her that he was trying to hold on. DeeDee stood up, slowly bent down, and kissed him. She whispered softly in his ear, "I love you baby. I will love you until the day I die." T.J.'s eyes began to smile and he slipped away from her forever.

Cool raindrops were beginning to dance upon the ocean's black, moonlit surface, but Dre continued to sit lifeless on the sandy beach. The same beach he played football on with T.J. and Domino when they were younger. The same beach he and Bianca walked and counted stars on many nights.

For the first time in his life, he was drinking alcohol. He sat alone at the edge of the shore gripping his fifth of white rum. He blamed himself for Bianca lying in the hospital with broken ribs and stitches from her pretty little head to her toes. He felt empty and alone. His parents, grandmother, Uncle, and two best friends were dead and he was personally responsible for one of those deaths.

He would never be able to forgive himself for Domino's death. Many times he tried justifying it with the fact that he threatened to bring down the organization. He was sure to wind up in prison for the rest of his life, if Angel didn't kill him first. Not to mention Bianca finding out about his other identity and leaving him for sure. Even though it looks like he may lose her anyway.

Dre wanted to stand up and walk into the ocean until all of his pains were gone. He felt as if he had no reason to live. He didn't feel worthy of life because he had ruined so many others, when all he wanted to do was help. Burying T.J. was hard for him. T.J. apparently contracted HIV from a blood transfusion given to him after he was shot years earlier with a bullet meant for Domino at a nightclub. It seems that the friends, who loved each other like brothers, would ultimately be responsible for each other's deaths.

He felt horrible about his sister and his best friend having to hide their love for each other for so many years. He never thought T.J. wasn't good enough for DeeDee, he just didn't want his lifestyle to hurt her. He knew he had been selfish and he felt as if DeeDee would hate him for a long time. He only wanted to protect his sister, just as he promised that he would.

Dre hoped that things would finally be nearing the end. DeeDee and her task force were swooping down on Angel and his cartel at that very moment at his Key West beach home. With the help of Dre, she was finally able to get enough information on the Sanchez organization to get an indictment. Dre lay back in the sand allowing the rain to drench him. He was too drunk to move.

The blazing heat of the morning sun and sounds of seagulls woke him up. He couldn't believe he slept on the beach all night. He rushed home to shower and change before he headed for the hospital to see Bianca, but first he planned to stop by DeeDee to get the information on the bust last night. He had expected her to call last night but he wasn't home. He tried calling her at the house but he didn't get an answer, so he decided to try the office. As he was dialing her number at the bureau he glanced over at the television. CNN was reporting on the unsuccessful raid at the Sanchez mansion in the Florida Keys. He quickly turned up the volume. Reports showed that eight agents and five of Sanchez's men were killed in the attempt. At the same time, Sgt. Milligan, DeeDee's supervisor answered her direct line.

"Tom…where is my sister," Dre asked in a nervous voice. Sgt. Milligan hesitated.

"Dre…they've got her. We don't know where she is, but we're trying to locate them now. We think Sanchez may have fled the country and has DeeDee hostage," he said in a concerned voice. Dre had met Tom a couple of years earlier at DeeDee's house, so the two of them had become acquainted with each other, but of course Tom had no idea that Dre was connected with Angel.

"What do you mean you don't know where my sister is? Why in the hell aren't you out there looking for this fucking Columbian instead of answering this damn phone," he shouted, as he slammed the phone down. Dre was relieved that she was not one of the agents that was killed last night, but how long would she remain alive once Angel realized that she was his sister, if it wasn't already too late. He was out of control. He began kicking and throwing things around the house. Angel had to be stopped. He paced up and down the floor, thinking and praying, praying and thinking. Suddenly his phone began to ring. Dre ran and picked it up...

"You're not a smart man Lanier and neither is your sister," snarled Angel.

"Where is she Sanchez? Is she...," he paused.

"Dead? Is she dead...no, not yet anyway," he toyed with Dre.

"What do you want Angel? Is it me? Is it the money? I have ten million of your dollars, and 15 million of my own. It's yours, I will give it all to you, just don't hurt my sister," he cried. Dre didn't care about showing emotion anymore, he just wanted DeeDee back and safe. "Please, put her on, I just want to make sure she's alright."

"Dre," said a frightened DeeDee. "I love you big brother."

"Hang on baby sis. You know I'm on my way."

"No! Don't come, he's going to kill you," she interrupted. Angel snatched the phone from her.

"10 o'clock tonight, on your boat," said Angel. Meet me about five miles south of the inlet. If you don't see me there, just sit and wait. And Dre... no FED's, or you, your little sister, and your hot little girlfriend will die tonight.

Dre sat at the graves of his parents for hours. He always use to find peace here, but today he was unable to.

"I'm so sorry," he cried over and over. All these years everything that he had ever worked for always centered around his family, but tonight is the true test. Tonight he has to bring his sister home safely and bring Angel down for good. He promised his parents one last time, that he would try to fix things.

The Miami division of the Drug Enforcement Agency had been sitting in the briefing room all morning, plotting out their next move and trying to locate Sanchez and Sgt. Snipes. The task force was viewing files and files of slides of photos that had been taken of the cartel for years.

Sgt. Milligan sat staring at the hundreds of slides trying to find some type of leads that could help him find his colleague and friend, but he could not detect any new clues. Frustrated and exhausted he threw his cup of coffee at the projection screen. Slide after slide came and went. Then suddenly, he caught a glimpse of something shocking.

"Wait go back to that slide," he shouted, as he stood up in astonishment. "Zoom in on the boat," he said, as he walked towards the screen to get a closer look.

"What is it Tom," asked Lt. Aikens, his superior officer.

"Oh my God, you little bastard you," he whispered to himself, as he grabbed his jacket and stormed out of the room. Lt. Aikens ran after him. He'd known Tom for over 15 years so he trusted his hunches. He caught up with Tom in the elevator.

"Talk to me Tom, what do you know?" The elevator reached the lobby floor of the headquarters building and Tom got off. He slowly turned around and looked at his curious friend.

"I know who knows where we can find Sanchez and Sgt. Snipes. I just need to get to him before he gets them all killed," he shouted as he ran towards his car.

Bianca slowly opened her eyes, still groggy from her pain medication. As her eyes focused she saw Dre sitting quietly beside her bed. His head was resting in his hands and his knuckles were bleeding from him pounding his fist on the pavement in anger.

"Andre," Dre looked up at her, she looked like an angel to him, and he loved her so much. He reached out for her awaiting hand and held on for dear life.

"How are you feeling baby," he asked as he leaned over and kissed her gently.

"Ready to go home to my family," she replied. Little did she know Dre had already arranged for her discharge from the hospital. He knew Angel meant business and he didn't want to take any more chances with his family. He had already made arrangements for Bianca and his family to get on the 7:30 flight to LA. She had a cousin that lived out there and promised to take care of them until they heard from him. Maggie was already waiting with the children downstairs for her.

"I'm not leaving without you Dre," she cried, holding on to his hand.

"Don't worry baby, I'll call you in a few days and let you know when we will be together again, okay? I need you to be strong and do what I tell you. It's for your own safety. Dre reached down on the floor and picked up a large duffle bag filled with money. He told her to keep this money for her and the children.

"Oh my God, there must be a million dollars in here honey," said Bianca, as she looked at him in amazement.

"There's actually two million dollars in here...More than enough for you, my sister Shannon, and the children to start over again if...if something should happen to me."

"No Dre, please don't say that. I can't bear to think about living without you.

"Bianca, there is no time baby, you have to go. Your plane leaves in an hour."

The two lovers held each other tight. The both knew that this may be the last time... Dre kissed Bianca's tears that were falling from her eyes. He himself found it difficult to let her go, but he was running out of time and he had work to do. He gave her one last look as he disappeared through the door.

GAME OVER

11:30, and still no sign of Angel. Dre paced the floor of his plush yacht that Angel had given to him seven months ago as a gift. He waited for Angel inside the bar area of the vessel. He could see every angle of the ship with the help of camera surveillance that had been installed by Angel. Dre, now drunk from the brandy which was heavily stocked in the bar, could hear the sounds of a smaller boat approaching. In walked Angel, but he was alone.

"Where is my sister, I have the money?" Angel began to laugh.

"Do you remember when I told you that you could never beat me at this game? You fucked up when you insisted on calling the shots. This is my game Lanier," shouted Angel.

"I don't give a damn about your game Sanchez, I never have! You drug me into this circus. All I wanted was to get out of something that I never asked to be a part of. This was your way of life, not mine." Dre picked up the bottle of brandy and took another drink. Angel reached into his pocket and pulled out a video tape.

"I want to show you something Lanier. Pay attention, I have a message for you," he said as he placed the tape into the VCR. There on the television was DeeDee and she had been beaten up pretty bad.

"You son of a bitch! What have you done with her," Dre cried, as he stood closer to the TV. He could see one of Angel's men grabbing her by her hair and trying to force her to speak into the camera. "No, no...Dee," he cried.

"You better say something bitch or else," shouted a voice in the background. DeeDee sat up in the chair refusing to cry, but her eyes showed fear. Suddenly someone struck her in her face knocking her from the chair. Dre grabbed his head and shouted, "Leave her alone you fuckers," he cried. Angel sat back in a chair smoking a cigarette while watching Dre suffer as he watched his sister being beaten and then brutally raped by his men.

"Dre," she shouted over and over...He could not watch anymore. He put his head down on the TV and sobbed like a baby.

"Don't stop watching Dre, the best part is about to happen," grinned Angel. Dre looked up at Angel and shook his head. He was afraid to look at the screen, but the screams of his sister drew his eyes to it. Suddenly someone else appeared into the camera, it was Angel. He took a gun from one of the men standing near and pointed it at DeeDee's head. "This is my favorite part," laughed Angel, as he got up and turned up the volume.

"No, Angel you didn't…no God, nooooo!" Angel stared into the camera as if he knew Dre would be watching.

"Say goodbye to your sister, Lanier," shouted Angel as he placed the gun to her head.

"I love you Dre," screamed DeeDee, as the sound of the cannon silenced her voice. Dre fell to his knees. He had just witnessed his sister being executed. He knew he would be next, and then Angel would not stop until he found his family and killed them one by one.

"Intense, wasn't it," said Angel. Dre snapped! He rose to his feet and roared as he charged Angel. The two rolled around the floor of the vessel, tearing away at each other. Dre's anger and pain gave him the strength to overpower Angel. He reached for a bottle that was lying near the entangled men.

"Bam!" Dre struck Angel several times in the face with the bottle. Laying semiconscious Angel remained outstretched on the cabin floor.

Dre struggled to reach the barstool to try to and lift himself up. Out of the corner of his eye he saw Angel's men on the surveillance camera climbing aboard the yacht wearing black wet suits. They apparently swam from a nearby boat. Dre knew they were coming for him. He reached on the bar for the bottle of brandy that he had been drinking before.

"Can you play chess Angel? I'm the pawn protecting my queen from the king. I have only one move to make to save her. Have a drink with me Angel. Let's drink to the end of a relationship, the end to the game." At least six of Angel's men were on board of the vessel heading toward the cabin. Dre opened a black box which held a detonator. While he waited for Angel to arrive he wired the boat with explosives just in case Angel double-crossed him. Dre took a deep breath and turned on the switch. He knew if Angel got off his boat alive Bianca and his family would die.

"It's not over until I say it's over," said Angel while he coughed up blood.

"No my friend, it's over...it's finally over," said Dre, as the boat exploded with a huge force. Flames and smoke shot up so high that it startled the coast guard who had been alerted by Sgt. Milligan.

He and the task force were on their way to apprehend Sanchez.

Money washed ashore for weeks in remembrance of the explosion. Bianca sat by the phone and waited for Dre to call her as he had promised, but she never got her call. She took the money that he had given her and opened a home for drug-addicted mothers and their babies. The "Lanier House," in honor of the man who died so many may live.

Thank you for reading Fatal Truce! Please leave a review on Amazon or Barnes & Noble and you can check out other titles from April Black and more at:

www.Printhousebooks.com

PRINTHOUSE BOOKS

Read it, Enjoy it, Tell a friend.

VIP INK Publishing Group, Incorporated.

Atlanta, GA.

www.PrintHouseBooks.com

www.ingramcontent.com/pod-product-compliance
Lightning Source LLC
Chambersburg PA
CBHW022008080426
42733CB00007B/518